To!

Sis. Glenda Duckett-Johnson

DON'T EAT THE BABY
The Characteristics of a Cannibalistic Church

Thank you for your prayers

and support.

God bless you!

TORRINO TRAVELL TRAVIS

Torrino Travell Travis

GODZCHILD PUBLICATIONS

Published by Godzchild Publications
a division of Godzchild, Inc.
22 Halleck St., Newark, NJ 07104
www.godzchildproductions.net

Printed in the United States of America 2018 - 1st Edition

Library of Congress Cataloging-in-Publications Data
ISBN: 978-1-942705-56-7

Scripture quotations taken from King James Version (KJV), New
International Version (NIV), International Children's Bible (ICB),
English Standard Version (ESV), Amplified Bible (AMP), Good News
Translation (GNT), New American Bible Revised Edition (NABRE)

2018

DEDICATION

This book is dedicated to the women whom God has placed in my life to love, encourage, support and pray for me – my wife, Sherina, my three daughters, Deonna, Janiyah, and Amiyah, my mother, Cassandra, and grandmother, Nadine.

ACKNOWLEDGEMENTS

I give all glory, honor, and recognition to my Lord and Savior Jesus Christ, for it is in Him that I live, move, and have my being.

I want to acknowledge my father in the gospel, Bishop Earley Dillard and home church, Shiloh Way of the Cross Church, in Martinsville, VA. You always told me that I could be and do anything in life, as long as I stayed in Christ.

To my Presiding Bishop, Bishop Alphonzo D. Brooks, Presiding Bishop Emeritus, Apostle Leroy H. Cannady, Sr., and the members of The Way of the Cross Church of Christ International, especially to our youth department that I have been blessed to lead for the last ten years, the International Youth for Christ. I am eternally gratefully for the family that God has given me as a member of this great organization.

To the church that God has blessed me to lead and pastor for the last nine years, City of Refuge Way of the Cross Church, Richmond, VA.

To my mentor, Dr. Sid Howard Credle, dean of the Hampton University School of Business (1999-2017). Thank you for hiring me right out of law school for my dream job and for appointing me to serve as your assistant for 13 years. This book would not have been written if it were not for your guidance and encouragement to research, write, and publish.

Lastly, I want to acknowledge all those who contributed to the writing and publishing of this book, including my wife, Sherina, transcriber and editor, Sonya Summerville, for SheEditsMyPaper, cover designer, Joy Miller for Injoy Designs, and to my publisher, Dr. Shaun Saunders and Godzchild Publications and to all the authors, bloggers, and scientists that provided invaluable information as I wrote this book.

PREFACE

A few years ago, I happened to log into my e-mail account and came across an interesting article about the top 10 most cannibalistic animals. Normally when I see these types of articles, I ignore them and go right into my e-mail. However, this time I decided to click on the article and read it. As I read about the various animals, I felt that God was beginning to show me how these patterns and traits could be displayed in many of our churches. At that point, I made some minor notes and moved on from it.

A few weeks later, I decided to teach on the subject at our church. Although I felt that I should do more with the bible study lesson, I filed the notes away. Last year, I was afforded the opportunity to speak during our Holy Convocation and 90th anniversary celebration of the founding of The Way of the Cross Church of Christ International. The Lord brought back to memory the message I had shared at our local church several years prior and pressed upon me to share it again.

Following the message, several people remarked that they had tried to take notes during the sermon, attempting to remember and match the various animals with the various traits in the church. Some pastors even requested a copy of my notes so that they could share the message with their local congregations. Thus, this book is an attempt to honor their request by providing my sermon notes in expanded form.

The book is not intended to be a critique of the church. By no means am I in a position to critique any church, pastor, or ministry. Likewise, I am not in any position to provide expert recommendations. My goal is to provide information for thought, dialogue, and perhaps provide practical solutions for addressing some of the issues presented through the various animals. Every pastor and church has or will likely be confronted by one or more of these animal spirits operating in our congregation.

In researching for this book, I was in constant awe of God's creation as I learned about the unique traits of each animal. In some cases, the animals discussed in this book exhibit similar explanations for their cannibalistic behaviors. However, each had its own unique trait or variation. Some may read and conclude that another animal better depicts the particular behavior manifested in the church. You may find that the cause as well as the solutions to the various issues can be solved with similar strategies. For those who may have heard the original sermon, you will find that some of the animals and issues have changed.

I am also inspired by the numerous authors, bloggers, and writers, who have written extensively on each subject and provided practical solutions to address the various issues confronting our churches. Through my research, I learned that churches of all ages, sizes, and denominations are confronting similar issues. With more prayer, research, and dialogue across denominational lines, I believe that we can confront these issues better together rather than in isolation.

My hope is that because of this book, you will become more aware and recognize the issues within your congregation and with the help of God learn how to fight off the cannibalistic traits in your church. Paul reminds us that, "We wrestle not against flesh and blood, but against powers, principalities, and rulers of darkness in high places" (Ephesians 6:12, King James Version). We must never forget that we are indeed engaged in spiritual warfare. Yet we are not to lie down and accept casualties or defeat. Never forget the words of Jesus Christ, "Upon this rock, I will build my church, and the gates of hell shall not prevail against it" (Matthew 16:18, King James Version). While Christ never promised that his church would avoid attack, he did guarantee that the enemy would not succeed against it.

Moreover, my prayer is for those who have perhaps been attacked or victimized by a cannibalistic spirit within a particular church. No matter what you have experienced, please do not give up on God, nor His church. Recognize that while the devil's job is to steal, kill, destroy, Jesus Christ has come to give you life, and to give it to you more abundantly. Just because we may have been attacked or wounded, does not give us an excuse to lie down and just die. God wants to plant you in the right garden in order for you to live, grow, thrive, and serve.

LAMENTATIONS 2:20 NIV
"Look, LORD, and consider:
Whom have you ever treated like this?
Should women eat their offspring,
the children they have cared for?
Should priest and prophet be killed
in the sanctuary of the Lord?

LAMENTATIONS 4:10
With their own hands compassionate women
have cooked their own children,
who became their food
when my people were destroyed.

TABLE OF
Contents

INTRODUCTION

²⁴ *And it came to pass after this, that Benhadad king of Syria gathered all his host, and went up, and besieged Samaria.* ²⁵ *And there was a great famine in Samaria: and, behold, they besieged it, until an ass's head was sold for fourscore pieces of silver, and the fourth part of a cab of dove's dung for five pieces of silver.* ²⁶ *And as the king of Israel was passing by upon the wall, there cried a woman unto him, saying, Help, my lord, O king.* ²⁷ *And he said, If the* LORD *do not help thee, whence shall I help thee? out of the barnfloor, or out of the winepress?* ²⁸ *And the king said unto her, What aileth thee? And she answered, This woman said unto me, Give thy son, that we may eat him to day, and we will eat my son to morrow.* ²⁹ *So we boiled my son, and did eat him: and I said unto her on the next day, Give thy son, that we may eat him: and she hath hid her son.* ³⁰ *And it came to pass, when the king heard the words of the woman, that he rent his clothes; and he passed by upon the wall, and the people looked, and, behold, he had sackcloth within upon his flesh.* ³¹ *Then he said, God do so and more also to me, if the head of Elisha the son of Shaphat shall stand on him this day.* ³² *But Elisha sat in his house, and the elders sat with him;*

*and the king sent a man from before him: but ere the
messenger came to him, he said to the elders, See ye
how this son of a murderer hath sent to take away
mine head? look, when the messenger cometh, shut
the door, and hold him fast at the door: is not the
sound of his master's feet behind him? 33 And while
he yet talked with them, behold, the messenger came
down unto him: and he said, Behold, this evil is of the
LORD; what should I wait for the LORD any longer?*

–(2 Kings 6:24-33, King James Version)

W hen we think about cannibalism, a lot of us who were born prior to the 1990s may remember a man by the name of Jeffrey Dahmer, also known as 'The Milwaukee Cannibal'. He was a serial killer, a sex offender, who committed rape, murder, and was responsible for the dismemberment of 17 men and boys, between 1978 and 1991. Many of his later murders also involved necrophilia (having sex with dead people). Dahmer was diagnosed with Borderline Personality Disorder. Although he was found to be sane, he was sentenced to 17 life sentences for his acts. Ultimately, he was killed in prison.

As we examine the highlighted scriptural passage in the beginning of this introduction, it is clear in 2 Kings 6 that famine has hit Israel. This famine did not come because God could not provide rain, crops, or a harvest. Instead, Moses warned God's people that if they turned away from God in order to worship idols, then there would be perversion in the land and God would consequently decided to hold back the rain. Not only would God hold back the rain, but it would eventually get to a point where mothers would have to eat the flesh of their own children in order to survive.

Deuteronomy 28:57 confirms this conclusion when the writer says, "And toward her young one that cometh out from between her feet, and toward her children which she shall bear: for she shall eat them for want of all *things* secretly in the siege and straitness, wherewith thine enemy shall distress thee in thy gates" (King James Version). Ezekiel picks up from these words, and extends this harsh penalty to the fathers in his summation: "Therefore the fathers shall eat the sons in the midst of thee, and the sons shall eat their fathers; and I will execute judgments in thee, and the whole remnant of thee will I scatter into all the winds" (Ezekiel 5:10, King James Version). So, in this particular passage of scripture, we see that the predictions of old have come to pass. Perversion, idolatry, witchcraft is in the land, and Israel is in trouble.

How could a person eat their own child? Not another person, or another person's child, but how can one consume what they carried in their own womb? How can you swallow the very thing you gave birth to, and nursed? To not only kill the child, but then, to turn around and eat the child? This is unfathomable to imagine! Of course, many mothers have opted not to continue their pregnancy. Some have had to abort for medical purposes, and unplanned pregnancies are real situations that many people have to deal with. However, these women have not

xviii | DON'T EAT THE BABY: THE CHARACTERISTICS OF A CANNIBALISTIC CHURCH

carried the child full-term, labored to give birth to said child, and developed a bond with this child. Others in the Old Testament were aware of the practice of child sacrifices. For them, this was the highest form of worship to a deity, but again, their sacrifice was rooted in their belief. It wasn't seen as consuming in desperation the very thing you conceived in passion.

Consider mothers like Susan Smith. In 1995, due to mental illnesses and drug addiction, Susan Smith became overwhelmed with stress and killed her own child. Sadly, it is not uncommon to hear in the news how a mother may have left their child in the car while they went to work or went shopping, only to find that the child had suffocated in the car. Some of us even remember our own mothers and fathers telling us, "Boy, I'm gonna kill you if you don't get it together." Perhaps you were an angel growing up, but some of us may remember, Mom and Dad saying those infamous words of terror and fear: "I brought you in this world and I'll take you out." However, in none of these situations did the mother turn around and actually eat their own child.

I just need to revisit this question because it is appalling to me when I read the text using my full imagination: how does one kill, cook, season, tear, cut, and then consume their own child, limb by limb, bite by bite, chew by chew? We're not talking about chicken, we're not talking about beef, we're not talking about fish, we're not talking about pork, but your own flesh and blood? The child that came out of your womb is now to be put back in your body through your mouth, down your throat, through your stomach, and then excreted from your body; for you to then turn around and look at your own feces, and say, "That was once my child."

Questions such as, "Do you season the child? Do you prepare side dishes—collard greens, mashed potatoes? Do you fix a dessert? Do you drink water, wine or some other drink to wash it down? How do you live with yourself after you have consumed your own child?"

The more I asked myself these questions, the more I began to take these questions more seriously. I began researching the characteristics of cannibalistic animals and found how their traits have crept into our churches. These cannibalistic animals are spirits that have permeated our churches. And so, the question that God laid on my heart, "Are we a cannibalistic church?"

People often say, "Sticks and stones may break my bones, but words will never hurt me." That's a lie. You can heal a broken arm, but some of us remember the words from our childhood, even to this day. We've allowed actions and intolerance, impatience, lack of prayer, lack of teaching, lack of role models and mentors, make our church a cannibalistic body.

Many people have joined our churches and it has become the worst experience of their lives. Why? Because the cannibalistic spirit has permeated our churches. These babes in Christ are left wondering, "Why did you birth me, only to turn around and kill me...and then eat me?

CHAPTER 1

THE CAT

Imagine being a young adult. You're new to the area, and you are here because of college or because you were hired for a new job. You decide to visit a well-known church with a sizable membership—one that is steeped in rich tradition. After visiting for a few weeks you notice something interesting. You do not see too many people your age at the church. Upon closer examination, you observe the section for the older men and women in the church, the section for the middle-aged couples, and a small section in the church where the children and youth tend to sit.

As you look around, you find very few young adults in the service. One Sunday after service, the pastor states how glad he is to have you worship with them. He hopes that you will stay, become active in the ministry, and then he says it, "Help us win back our young adults." During your conversation with the pastor, you learn that some of the young adults are away in college, while others have moved away for employment opportunities elsewhere. Furthermore, you notice the change of countenance and the tone in his voice shift as the pastor shares stories of those that the church had helped send to college, but upon graduation, and returning home, decided to attend a different church in town. Others got married at their home church, but decided to find a different church with their spouse or attend their spouse's home church.

The pastor goes on to share other stories of teenagers that were saved, strong, and on fire for God but as young adults completely strayed away, changed their beliefs or perhaps got caught up in situations that pulled them out the church (issues like drugs, crime, unwed-pregnancy, and divorce). The pastor strongly believed that if he could get a core of young adults to stay then he could perhaps draw others back into the ministry. After listening intently to the pastor, the young-adult responds by saying these words, "Pastor, I believe you have a cat problem in your church!"

Unlike all of the other cannibalistic animals in this book, the cat is the only domesticated animal that is routinely kept as a pet. This seemingly nice, soft, and cuddly pet makes the list as one of the top cannibalistic animals. The cat is unique in that the mother cat "queen" has been observed to eat its own kittens. As a relatively common behavioral disorder, cannibalism accounts for 12.5% of pre-weaning kitten losses.

In rare cases, mother cats may eat their newborn kitten by accident when trying to cut the umbilical cord or by eating the placenta. Mother cats are also known to intentionally destroy an inferior or malformed kitten or to eat a stillborn kitten. However, the most common, intentional form of cat cannibalism is caused by maternal aggression which may be activated by fear, anxiety, anger or a perceived threat to the mother's survival. In this case, eating a newborn kitten appears to be associated with having a large litter, a second pregnancy, being a highly nervous first-time mother, or an illness in the kitten. Cat cannibalism can also be provoked by the stress of finding an appropriate nesting area or extreme malnourishment of the mother cat. Regardless of the reason, the reality is the same—the mother cat may resort to eating one of its own newborn kittens.

According to a recent Barna Group survey, church attendance and impressions of the church are the lowest in recent history. The report found the following:

- Only 2 in 10 Americans under 30 believe attending a church is important or worthwhile (an all-time low).
- 59% percent of millennials raised in a church have dropped out of church.
- 35% of millennials have an *anti-church* stance, believing the church does more harm than good.
- Millennials are the least likely age group of anyone to attend church (by far).

Note: for this chapter, young adults and Millennials will be used interchangeably. However, the issue of young adults not being represented in our congregations actually pre-dates Millennials. Young adults are roughly defined as those between the ages of 18-30, perhaps even as old as 35 years old. Millennials are defined, depending on the author, as those born between the time frame of the late 1970's or early 1980's and the late

1990's or the year 2000. Based on the range in one's date of birth, a millennial at the time of this book would possibly fall somewhere between the ages of 18-40 years old. Consequently, because Millennials are the current young adults, they will be referred to interchangeably in this chapter[1].

Even though there is some debate over the definition of a "dropout" and the exact percentage of young adults who have dropped out of church in recent years, most studies do share a common concern over the number of young adults that leave the church, albeit perhaps temporarily. Further, to complicate matters, there is no consensus as to the reasons for such attendance figures for young adults.

Several articles, listed for your further reading at the end of this chapter, provide anywhere from five to fifteen reasons why young adults do not attend church on a regular basis. It is not important to assess the merits of each point, but this chapter will discuss the most common reasons why young adults leave the church. Setting aside young adults who may leave the church temporarily or inconsistent attendance, Lifeway reports, of those who

---

[1] As this book was being written, the Pew Research Center issued guidelines defining Millennials as those born between 1981 and 1996. The Pew Research Center considered such historic events such as 9-11 and the "Great Recession" as defining moments for Millennials. It also considered inventions such as Google, Social Media, and various Apple products such as the iPod, iTunes, iPhone, and iPads as technology that differentiates the generations. Consequently, some have referred to this new generation as iGen. Based on this definition, Millennials are transitioning out of the ranks of being considered young adults with Post-Millennials or Generation Z entering the years of being considered a young adult.

dropped out, 97 percent stated it was for life changing reasons such as:

- They simply wanted a break from church (27 percent).
- They moved to attend college (25 percent).
- Their work made it impossible or difficult to attend (23 percent).

When reading these statistics, it is easy to dismiss the low attendance by young adults as merely the consequence of normal patterns of life. Church can fall into the fallacy of reasoning that young adults are not in the church because youth will stray away and eventually find their way back to church once they settle down, marry, and start a family. This may be true for some, but research indicates that Millennials are not as apt to "settle down," get married, or have a desire to return to church later in life. However, research also indicates a much larger, troubling trend that goes beyond the "drop-out phenomenon" as merely a typical stop on the cycle of life. Studies are showing that an alarming emerging number of young adults have a high level of disillusionment (distrust/disdain), dissatisfaction, and detachment with the church that may not be cured with old age and the passing of time.

DISILLUSIONMENT

One of the most common reasons why young adults are leaving the church is disillusionment. Disillusionment is defined as "a feeling of disappointment resulting from the discovery that something is not as good as one believed it to be." In general, Millennials are skeptical of institutions, but specifically when it comes to the church. Their perception is that the church is full of unwelcoming, judgmental, and hypocritical members. They may have seen and heard church fights and politics play out in the pews. Repeated scandals in the media involving the clergy and finances, infidelity, and sexual abuse has created both a distrust in the church, and in many cases a complete disdain for Christianity.

Author Frank Powell states, "Millennials are not looking for perfect people…Jesus already handled that. Millennials are looking for people to be real and honest about struggles and temptations." Powell further writes, "Millennials value transparency and authenticity."

A few years ago, Food Lion, a grocery store chain, had a scandal involving its meat and its handling. However, the chain was able to rehabilitate its brand through transparency by allowing the customer to see into the meat department. Perhaps if the church returns to a level of authenticity and transparency it can rehabilitate its image before it's too late.

DISSATISFACTION

Another theme in understanding why Millennials are leaving the church is their level of dissatisfaction with how the church applies Christianity to everyday living. Young adults do not want to hear bible stories unless it can be connected to helping them better understand and navigate life in their career, home, and community. Young adults are dissatisfied with a Christianity that is only preached but is not practiced.

As a politically and socially conscious age-group, Millennials are bored with the idea of only having church for church people without any meaningful impact on the outside world. Millennials want a form of Christianity that is not a mere monument to be revered but a movement that brings about positive change in the world around them. Millennials are not looking to separate from culture and society but to impact it. Millennials understand that the mission field is not just a third world country, but the classroom, board room, courthouse, athletic field, and big screen. In many cases, Millennials are not leaving the church because they have lost confidence in it, but because they believe that the church and Christianity can do and be about so much more than a service on Sunday mornings.

Further, Millennials want clear answers to tough questions. The generation of accepting what mother says because "she said so" no longer exists. With young people being more educated and having access to information on television, the internet, and social media, the church can no longer gloss over or give tongue-in-cheek answers to difficult questions. It is not that Millennials are hostile to doctrine and standards, but they are hostile to man-made doctrines and traditions that cannot be supported by scripture. Millennials would rather hear that some stances are good policy, practice, or tradition, instead of being misapplied interpretations of scripture to support something that is not biblical.

It is no coincidence that our current generation replete with reality television, natural hair, natural food, natural music, and natural medicines also wants a pure Christianity and an authentic worship experience without unnecessary additives, preservatives, artificial fillers, or colors. If there is no need for it – don't include it. If it is not beneficial – take it out. If it is actually going to harm me in the long run, tell me now so I can stop using it. If it is fake, then don't lead me to believe that it is real. Often it is not the product that is the issue, but the transparency and the labeling on the product.

As one author stated, "Millennials are seeking a church that is not merely a gathering place but a scattering place that goes out and fulfills the great commission of Jesus Christ". Thus, the Millennial disappointment with the church is not because of low expectations but because they love God, their faith, and the church, and want to see it reach its full potential. Consequently, as we will address more later, there is a need for the church to harness and unleash the young adults to do more in ministry.

DISCONNECTED

Millennials are leaving the church because they feel disconnected. Perhaps it's no coincidence that the generation of text messaging and social media would raise the issue of connectivity, community, and accessibility. For many young adults, the reason they leave the church is simple – they do not feel wanted or needed by the church.

This notion of disconnection manifests itself in numerous ways. Some young adults state that the church does not focus on their age group. Most churches have well-organized ministries and facilities that cater to children and youth. However, when youth graduate high school, they are immediately pooled into the masses with all other adults, ranging from 18 to 80 years old. There are unique needs for young adults as they transition into adulthood such as college, career, marriage, family, as well as financial firsts including the purchase of their first home and car. Where does the young adult fit in if they are no longer children, but do not have all of the adult issues and responsibilities of their parents and grandparents?

Students who go away to college often come home during breaks or after graduation to find that the church has moved on without them and that they are an outsider visiting. The church has to make a concerted effort to pray over and remain connected to its youth who go away to college or serve in the military. How the church treats a student during their first semester away will have a major impact on whether they return to worship and serve at that church after graduation.

Disconnect also happens when the church fails to provide young adults with meaningful opportunities to serve in ministry. A lot of churches miss out on the innovation, energy, and capabilities of young adults. Often still seeing them as "the kid from Sunday school or children's church", but fail to see how God has raised them up to be leaders in the church.

King David had a similar experience with his brothers at the Valley of Elah. David's brothers had witnessed Samuel anoint David the future king of Israel. However, when David came to bring food to his brothers, they remarked,

> *"And Eliab his eldest brother heard when he spake unto the men; and Eliab's anger was kindled against David, and he said, Why camest thou down hither? and with whom hast thou left those few sheep in the wilderness? I know thy pride, and the naughtiness of thine heart; for thou art come down that thou mightest see the battle. [29] And David said, What have I now done? Is there not a cause?"*
>
> —(1 Samuel 17:28-29, King James Version)

Contrastingly, when Saul heard about David's inquiry into the reward for killing Goliath, Saul discouraged David but did not completely dismiss David. As David shared with Saul his experiences as a shepherd with the lion and bear, and Saul realizing that for 40 days no one had stepped up to the plate to fight Goliath, Saul decided to give David a chance. Initially placing his armor on David, David rejected Saul's armor opting to fight with his own, more familiar weapons, of a sling shot and five rocks. In the end, David was successful in killing Goliath and giving Israel victory over the Philistines that day.

Setting aside Saul's later insecurity, jealousy, and mishandling of his greatest asset, David, we can glean several lessons from Saul's initial encounter with David. First, rather than dismiss David, Saul was willing to hear David out. Second, when David refused to fight with Saul's armor, Saul allowed him to fight with his own weapons. How many pastors and churches have been staring at Goliaths for years, looking to the same people for the same unfruitful solutions but ignoring a "David", anointed by God, to bring victory and deliverance to his people? David's brothers had the position, experience, and resources to fight but did not have the courage or passion to fight for the cause of Israel.

As churches, we have two choices with our young, passionate, fearless, and anointed Davids: we can either run them away like David's brothers did, or we can give them a chance and allow them to use their own methods as Saul did. Look at how many Philistines David killed from the time he was anointed king until the time he became king at the age of 30. It is time for you to release your Davids!

Many young adults can see how their hard work, dedication, and consistency can advance their career in their secular profession but are required to sit on the sidelines in church because they are not married, old enough, or perceived to lack spiritual maturity.

In many churches a young adult is put on hold or told to wait on serving in key positions until they are "married" and "more" settled. However, Paul writing to the church in Corinth views singleness as an asset to ministry. First Corinthians 7: 29-35

"What I mean, brothers and sisters, is that the time is short. From now on those who have wives should live as if they do not; those who mourn, as if they did not; those who are happy, as if they were not; those who

buy something, as if it were not theirs to keep; those who use the things of the world, as if not engrossed in them. For this world in its present form is passing away. I would like you to be free from concern. An unmarried man is concerned about the Lord's affairs—how he can please the Lord. But a married man is concerned about the affairs of this world— how he can please his wife— and his interests are divided. An unmarried woman or virgin is concerned about the Lord's affairs: Her aim is to be devoted to the Lord in both body and spirit. But a married woman is concerned about the affairs of this world—how she can please her husband. I am saying this for your own good, not to restrict you, but that you may live in a right way in undivided devotion to the Lord."

–(New International Version)

Thus many churches are missing out on the best years of a person's life to perhaps put them to work in the church. Without having to balance as many responsibilities at home, many single young adults have the heart, mind, ability, and time to serve more in church.

Rather than remain constantly frustrated or seen as a problem, many young adults move on to other ministries or professions that will allow them to exercise their gifts and talents thereby fulfilling their calling and destiny.

The final form of disconnect occurs between the pulpit and the pews. Young adults want more than just a weekly lecture or a monologue. Research indicates that young adults are looking for role models, mentors, and people who are willing to take the time to disciple them.

THE CAT | 13

They are seeking church leaders who are approachable and accessible. They are seeking leaders who view them as more than a "number sign" and "dollar sign" in the church. As one remarked, I don't care what you know until I know that you care about me. Young adults are crying out, "We have questions, we want biblical answers, but no one is willing to take the time to teach us!"

Rae'Jean Spears
Yesterday at 8:16 PM · ⊘

Millennials are not leaving the church because of God...we're leaving because of YOU.
We're leaving because we have to get through your 5 armor bearers & 2 watchmen just to shake your hand after service. We're leaving because you care more about the fact we're wearing pants instead of a skirt than our salvation. We're leaving because you will preach till you're blue in the face, but can't genuinely speak when we see you out in public. We're leaving because you preach for 10 minutes, hoop+holler for 20, but can't engage with us on ANY of our questions about theology. We're leaving because you can take up 3 offerings to reach your goal, but you're NEVER in the community doing service.

Need I continue? This generation IS a generation after God's own heart....along with sound doctrine & real community. But, we are NOT here to play these fake & phony games. We will get our Bibles & meet in a living room, coffee shop, or park before we sit under some of this "leadership" today. 👊
#WeAreOVERIt ²

Growing up with unlimited access to computers and technology, Millennials have developed a hands-on, interactive style of learning that finds monologues and

---

² Reprinted by permission of Rae'Jean Spears.

lectures to be boring and ineffective. Millennials are looking for authentic believers who live out their faith in their daily lives and are transparent and open in sharing their failures, struggles, and successes as a Christian. Authenticity does not mean preaching in blue jeans and tee-shirts or having the latest technology in the church. Millennials are looking for less preaching but more teaching, coaching, pure worship experiences and conversations as they search for biblical answers to life's questions while creating a genuine connection with God.

ELIHU

In the book of Job, we read the dialogue between Job and his friends—Eliphaz the Temanite, Bildad the Shuhite, and Zophar the Naamathite. For 30 chapters we read the seesaw conversation these men have with Job as they all attempt˛ to understand why Job had lost everything. However, in chapter 32 we learn of a fifth person who had been in the room the entire time but had not spoken.

"So Elihu son Barakel the Buzite said this: I am young, and you are old. That is why I was afraid to tell you what I know. I thought, 'Older people should speak. Those who have lived many years should teach wisdom.' But it is the spirit of in a person that gives him understanding. It is the breath of God All-Powerful in him. It is not just older people who are wise. Older people are not the only ones who understand what is right...No, I also will speak. I will also tell what I know. I am full of words. And the spirit in me causes me to

speak. I am like wine that has been bottled up. I am ready to burst like a new leather bag for holding wine. I must speak. Then I will feel relief. I must open my mouth and answer. I will be fair to everyone. I don't know how to flatter. If I did, God my Maker, would quickly take me away."

—(International Children's Bible)

Although we do not know the exact age of Elihu, he poetically expresses the sentiments of many Millennials and young adults. They have tried to wait, be respectful, and listen. However, they cannot deny the anointing on their lives and the ministries contained in them. They are like wine that has been bottled up and ready to burst. The question is *will the church stop, listen, and give them the opportunity to speak?* In reading the conclusion of the book of Job, we learn that neither Job nor his friends challenged or refuted anything that Elihu said. In fact, even when God chastised Job and his friends, God did not require Elihu to repent for speaking incorrectly. Perhaps this young man, who waited his turn really did know the mind of God and spoke His words truthfully. How great could our churches be if pastors and church leaders could learn this lesson from Elihu?

Perhaps in reading this chapter you've become more aware of the heart and mind of Millennials and desire to bring an end to the cannibalistic cat in your church. Below are a few practical tips:

1. Develop an affirmative action plan to train and place younger people in key positions of leadership. Is there

a biblical reason why a Millennial cannot serve as a head of a major ministry within your church, serve in an ecclesiastical position as deacon, missionary, or minister, or even on the board of trustees?

2. If Millennials can be sent around the world to fight wars, be hired to leadership positions in corporate America (sometimes overseeing more people and more money than they would in the church), or even as entrepreneurs, launch billion-dollar businesses, surely, they can have a meaningful role in ministry. If a young adult does stay or return home from college, do not put them in a token position—giving them a nice title, but no actual authority—or leave them on the sideline.

3. Institute a youth advisory board that meets on a regular schedule with the pastor and church leadership team. Give voice to the young adults in a constructive and structured way without being defensive or closed-minded to their ideas and opinions. Even though they may not have the most money or seniority in the church, they are members of the church, they are the future of the church, and should have a voice in the church.

4. Create or revamp the church singles' ministry or young adult ministry. The singles' ministry should not be focused solely on preparing people to get married in the future, but on how to live saved and successful lives in their present time and status. Age-appropriate Bible studies can be specially crafted to deal with questions about bible and church doctrine in an open, honest, and judgment-free manner. In addition, seminars and

workshops can be planned to help with decision making, career planning and preparation, financial literacy, home ownership, Christian dating and marriage. Likely, this will be the ministry that the church can utilize to be innovative in developing outreach and evangelistic events and activities for the church.

5. Implement a campus ministry for both in-bound and out-bound college students. While it is true that many young people intentionally look forward to all the vices that come with college, many, on the other hand, desire to remain connected to the church, maintain their faith, and live out their Christians values while away from home. However, without pre-college mentoring, accountability, prayer, and care, many churches allow their college students to fall through the cracks. Someone must have a heart for the college student and be willing to stay in contact with them, send an encouraging word, send a care packet, and help them navigate through the jungle of college. For many in the congregation, out of sight means out of mind. If a church wants to retain young adults, especially those that it sends away to college, it must make remaining connected to them a priority. Likewise, as students return home for the weekend, holidays or the summer, it is important that they are made to feel that their church home is still their home. Even if a church has to fill a role in their absence, are they allowed to continue working in those areas when they come home from college? Can

they still work in the nursery or children's church, sing on the choir or praise team, or serve in the media ministry? If it appears that the church has moved on without them, chances are they will move on from the church after they graduate.

6. For in-bound students, it will be important to craft a well-defined "watch-care" policy. Not just for college students but for others who might temporarily be in the area for work, family, or military service. Even if you are not in a college town, you never know who might be willing to commute an hour or more to attend services at your church. Just because a student comes to your church from a different ministry does not mean that they cannot contribute and serve in your ministry. Though they may have loyalty to their home church, go home frequently, or may not be able to attend every event at your church, chances are you are missing out on someone that God has sent to your ministry for a season to help you. Flexibility is key and demanding tithes is a turnoff. While it is a possibility they may remain permanently at your church, chances are they will go home or move on to another city. A church's mission is not to recruit members but to support the Kingdom. Be there for them while they are there with you. Allow them to serve, assign someone to check on them regularly, occasionally provide them with a home-cooked meal, and put them to work in your ministry. God will reward you for caring and cultivating their ministry and gifts. Because of your efforts, many will remain in the

church, but also return home to be a greater asset to the ministry they previously left behind.

7. Strong youth ministries must be geared not just towards fellowship but salvation and discipleship. The enemy is going to try its best to pluck young people out, but we have to make sure we have thoroughly planted the word of God in them in the first place. A church must make sure that its youth have the gift of the Holy Ghost, along with a strong biblical foundation and personal relationship with Jesus Christ. Young people need role models and peers that will hold them accountable.

Discussion Questions

(1) What percentage of your active church membership is between the ages of 18-35?

(2) How many key leadership roles in your church are currently held by someone between the ages of 18-35?

(3) What activities and ministries are specifically targeted to young adults in your church?

(4) How can your church address the issues of disillusionment, disappointment, and disconnection with young adults?

(5) What type of mentoring or discipleship do you provide to young adults outside of traditional preaching or collective bible study?

(6) How well do you stay connected to your out-bound college students?

(7) How well do you integrate in-bound college students into your church?

(8) How easy is it for your college students to return home from break or graduation and get involved with your church?

(9) How is the Elihu dilemma dealt with in your church? What concerns do you have about entrusting young adults with major responsibilities in your church?

(10) How active is your church in the community? How engaged is your church in community activism, outreach, and ministry outside the "four walls" of the church?

References

Americans Divided on the Importance of Church
https://www.barna.com/research/americans-divided-on-the-importance-of-church/#.V-hxhLVy6FD

12 Reasons Millennials are OVER Church
http://www.recklesslyalive.com/12-reasons-millennials-are-over-church/

Study Analysis: 6 Reasons Why Only 2 in 10 Millennials Believe Church Attendance Is Important
https://www.christianpost.com/news/study-analysis-6-reasons-why-only-two-in-10-millennials-believe-church-attendance-is-important-116882/

Want millennials back in the pews? Stop trying to make church 'cool.'
https://www.washingtonpost.com/opinions/jesus-doesnt-tweet/2015/04/30/fb07ef1a-ed01-11e4-8666-a1d756d0218e_story.html?utm_term=.21bb06b9bcb9

Four More (BIG) Reasons Young Adults Quit Church
https://www.redletterchristians.org/four-more-big-reasons-young-adults-quit-church/

Seven Reasons Why Young Adults Quit Church
https://www.redletterchristians.org/seven-reasons-why-young-adults-quit-church/

Why don't young adults go to church?
https://themennonite.org/opinion/dont-young-adults-go-church/

Survey: Reasons Why Young Adults Quit Church
https://www.christianpost.com/news/survey-reasons-why-young-adults-quit-church-28813/

The Real Reasons Young Adults Drop Out of Church
http://www.christianitytoday.com/edstetzer/2014/december/real-reasons-young-adults-drop-out-of-church.html

10 Reasons Why People Don't Go To Church
http://www.petebrookshaw.com/2012/08/10-reasons-why-people-dont-go-to-church.html#.Wod48LynFY0

WHY YOUNG PEOPLE ARE GOING TO CHURCH AND WHAT CHANGES IT SHOULD BRING
http://mastersdust.com/2013/09/23/young-people-going-church-changes-bring/

5 Reasons Millennials Stay Connected to Church
https://www.barna.com/research/5-reasons-millennials-stay-connected-to-church/#.UkCXFT8wKSo

Not All Youth Leave Church! 3 Reasons Why They Stay
https://www.crosswalk.com/blogs/christian-trends/not-all-youth-leave-church-3-reasons-why-they-stay.html

Reaching out to young adults will screw up your church
https://www.christiancentury.org/blogs/archive/2012-05/reaching-out-young-adults-will-screw-your-church

Youth Pastors on Why Young Adults Stay in Church
https://www.crosswalk.com/blogs/christian-trends/not-all-youth-leave-church-3-reasons-why-they-stay.html

5 Reasons Why There Are No Millennials in Your Church
http://www.millennialevangelical.com/5-reasons-why-there-are-no-millennials-in-your-church/

10 Reasons Churches Are Not Reaching Millennials
http://frankpowell.me/ten-reasons-church-absent-millennials/

5 Reasons Why Not All Young Adults Leave the Church
https://www.crosswalk.com/church/youth-ministry/5-reasons-why-not-all-young-adults-leave-church.html

The Millennial Manual
By: Pastor Jay Patrick, 2018

CHAPTER 2

THE LOBSTER

The second cannibalistic animal is the lobster. Lobsters are those that will grow, but then they'll turn around and eat the young because they see the young as a threat to them.

Marine biologists are now finding the practice of adult lobsters eating young lobsters more common in the wild. With the recent rise in water temperatures, in places such as the Gulf of Maine, there has been a tremendous increase in the lobster population. When compounded with limited food supply, an increase in cannibalism amongst lobsters has been recorded. One research study found that young lobsters left in a bait trap were 90% more likely to be eaten by another lobster rather than another sea animal.

The commonality between the lobster in the wild and the lobster in captivity is this: when there is a limit, or competition, for food and space; the older, larger, established lobster will eat the younger, smaller, newcomer. In a tank, lobsters often have bans to keep them from hurting themselves and others, but in the wild they have absolutely nothing to restrain them.

As much as we pray for growth, read books, attend conferences, and have meetings on why the church is not growing, there are people in our congregations who really do not want the church to grow. They talk a good game about church growth, evangelism, outreach, and the Lord sending in laborers to aid in the ministry. However, when the Lord sends talented individuals to the church, these new members are met with the lobster spirit in the church.

A church with a lobster spirit has a reputation for being unfriendly and cliquish (no pun intended). Writer, Saleama A. Ruvalcaba writes, "Cliques are formed either knowingly or unknowingly and tend to ignore those who are looking for a place to call home." A study by Balswick and Layne identified four types of church cliques. "These are: the conjugal cluster (married couples); the Christian education cluster (the group that typically makes decisions on what is taught in the church); the established member cluster (long-standing members) and the prominent member cluster." While affinity groups, long-term friendships, and family bonds will exist in any church, it is important that new members are quickly integrated into the church family and not left feeling like they are intruders or not welcome to the church.

A cliquish church may in general be a very warm and friendly church, but to whom? In a cliquish church, members are very friendly to each other, show genuine love and concern towards each other, and may love to be around each other after service and at other times during the week. In many cases, this is ideal for a pastor to want the members to genuinely like and get along with each other and want to spend time with each other outside of church. We also teach our children to forsake the world and not to be unequally yoked with non-believers, so it is great when their closest friends are those in the church, right?

The issue with cliques in the church, however, is not the closeness of its members to each other, but a question of how long or through what hurdles must a new member endure before they become a part of this great family? One writer remarked, "We were welcomed with open arms, but kept at arms-length." Rob Edmondson writes that many people "just couldn't break into the already established groups within the church." In this culture, it may take years for people to feel included, find a place of service, or begin to lose the "new person" label within a church. Thus, the issue with cliques is not a problem with church members being close-knit but a question of inclusion and exclusion. How long and how hard is it for a new member to feel as though they are a part of the church family?

The reality is if new members are not integrated into the church family, as well as into service, and eventually into leadership roles, they will ultimately leave the church. No one wants to join a church and years later still feel like a visitor or an outsider.

The impact that this "visiting mentality" has on kids can be spiritually fatal. While adults may be more rooted in the faith and understand the importance of being a part of a church family, they will perhaps move on to another church in hopes of finding a genuine church family. However, for children, the cliques and constant moves may cause them, as adults, to never return back to the church. Ruvalcaba states, "Children already feel awkward in new situations so after they have made friends, they're learning and growing with their pastor, they have to leave a place they're thriving in because grown-ups don't know how to behave." Ruvalcaba adds, "The long-term effects of their feelings about church might not be known for years to come. When they become adults and no longer have an interest in church, we then shake our heads in confusion."

While cliques are a problem in many churches, it is likely that no church or pastor would ever admit that they are unfriendly or cliquish. Joe McKeever tells the story of an experience as a pastor where he shared two letters with his congregation. One letter was from a former member who recently moved away stating how much she missed her loving and friendly congregation. He went on to read another letter from a recent first-time visitor stating that they would never visit the church again because no one spoke to them and that the congregation was very unfriendly. The contrasting letters, he writes, make two vivid points. First, people who are integrated into the church may find the church to be very friendly and close-knit. However, the same church, to an outsider, first-time visitor, or new member may come across as cold, unfriendly, and unwelcoming.

McKeever concludes that the standard for determining whether a church is friendly, welcoming, or hostile and cliquish, will be the visitor. He writes, "The visitors are the authority on the friendliness of this congregation. Newcomers will learn in a heartbeat whether we are loving and welcoming. The fact seems to be that yes, we are friendly—to one another. Not to newcomers, first-timers, outsiders."

He further writes that the blame for an unfriendly cliquish church is sin and leadership. "As a result of the sinful, selfish heart, people drift away from loving other people and retreat into solitude. Then, even though man is naturally gregarious and craves fellowship, left to himself he will gravitate to a small band of buddies and then freeze out all outsiders who wish to break into the cluster."

McKeever, Ruvalcaba, LeClaire, and others agree that a church culture of unfriendliness and cliques is often an issue of church leadership. McKeever writes, "Let the pastors show themselves as friendly. Let them leave their inner sanctum (aka, "pastor's study") a good quarter-hour before every worship service and mill around inside the building greeting people, welcoming newcomers, and introducing them to others. In time, the people will do what their leaders do." Ruvalcaba states that it is important for leaders to constantly examine themselves, asking God to show them if they have shown favoritism or shunned others unfairly. LeClaire writes, "If you lead a church with cliques, talk to your staff and encourage them to discourage cliques at all levels. Help them understand the biblical value of developing a true community of believers who share one another's lives."

Cliques go against everything the Bible talks about in regard to reaching out to others and holding them in high esteem. Romans 12:16 says, "Live in harmony with one another. Do not be proud, but be willing to associate with people of low position" (New International Version). Philippians 2:3 states, "…in lowliness of mind let each esteem others better than themselves (King James Version). Verse 4 says, "Let each of you look out not only for his own interests, but also for the interests of others" (English Standard Version).

In some cases cliques are formed without knowledge but others are formed intentionally to preserve status, influence, control, and attention. Lobsters love to monopolize the time and the attention of the pastor. Lobsters see new members, their gifts and talents, not as an asset, but see it as a threat to the church. Lobsters see new singers as a threat, new musicians as a threat, new ministers as a threat, and even new young people as a threat. Lobsters will see young people, whether born in the church, saved during adolescence, or attending the church while in college as a threat to their position or space in the tank. Because of jealousy, envy, pride, insecurity, and competitiveness, a church with a lobster spirit will run away those whom God has sent to the ministry to help in an area that is desperately in need of assistance. If you are not a part of a certain family, clique, or have seniority in the church, you are not allowed to serve in the ministry. Lobsters, rather than slide over and share the bench, see new members as trying to take their entire seat, and refuse to move or share. Perhaps, paradoxically, the pastor and the congregation had been praying, for a while, for someone like them to join the ministry. However because of the culture and the construct of the church, it was unable to integrate or assimilate these new members into the ministry.

Even Jesus, in Mark 9:38, had to correct his disciples, for having a lobster spirit,

> *"And John answered him, saying, Master, we saw one casting out devils in thy name, and he followeth not us: and we forbad him, because he followeth not us. But Jesus said, Forbid him not: for there is no man which shall do a miracle in my name, that can lightly speak evil of me. For he that is not against us is on our part"*
>
> —(King James Version).

Scenario 1

Meet the Green Family. The Green Family recently moved into town because of a job opportunity. They are seasoned saints – Holy Ghost filled, faithful, talented, tithers who come to the church highly missed but recommended by their previous pastor. Dad is a minister, corporate executive, and is an excellent teacher, preacher, and worship leader. Mom is a stay-at-home mother who is an intercessor and altar worker. She loves working with children and during the school year is available to volunteer. Son is a talented musician and graphic designer. Daughter is an anointed singer and also has helped with children's church and the day care ministry at her previous church. Everyone rejoiced when God sent such a wonderful family into the church. However, within only a few months, the lobster spirit manifested itself in the church.

The ministers and Sunday school teachers did not want to add another minister to the rotation. For the last few weeks, Mom has been helping with the food pantry to help distribute food to the needy in the neighborhood. She recently made some suggestions on how to improve the ministry, based on her experience from her previous church. The head of the ministry quickly responded that they had been doing it this way "successfully" for a number of years and she did not welcome her trying to take over the ministry from her. Son is the best musician the church has but last Sunday he decided to sit down rather than fight over who would play the next song for the choir. The director indicated who would play which song during rehearsal, but when it came time to rotate, the drummer would not move. Daughter is frustrated because the other girls on the praise team are either family members or best friends. They often hang out after church and when they do, they often use it as a time to gossip or make fun of people at the church. Because Daughter has not known them as long nor cares to hang out with them if that is going to be the focus of the conversation, she is often labeled a stuck-up, snooty, or she "thinks she is better than everyone else." As a result, she really doesn't feel wanted or welcomed on the praise team and would rather stop singing than to sing with people that do not like her. The family really believes God sent them to the church to help, but is now trying to decide if they should go to a different church to serve or stay where they are but limit their participation.

Scenario 2

Sis. Brown is a sophomore at the local university. She is smart, talented, saved, and attractive. She is still a member of her home church, but while in school, she has made a commitment to serve and attend this church. Pastor believes she is an excellent role model in the church, especially to the young ladies. Pastor has gotten her to sing sermonic solos and even allowed her to sing on the choir even though she often can't make it to rehearsal because of her class schedule. Some of the young ladies in the church have become jealous and even started negative rumors about her because several of the young brothers in the church have a crush on her. They feel that the Pastor and First Lady favor her over the other young girls in the church. Recently, a parent confronts First Lady after service stating that she did not think it was fair that the church gets her to sing solos, miss choir rehearsal, and work with the youth ministry when she is not even a full member of the church. She goes on to say that her daughter is upset because she feels that there is double-standard and that the church favors this new girl over the ones that have been at the church all their lives. Shortly thereafter, Pastor shares with Sis. Brown that he may have to use her less because of the concerns expressed by some of the other parents. While Sis. Brown understands the importance of attending and serving in church while in school, she understands everyone's concern and is willing to be less visible and active in the ministry.

Scenario 3

Mother Reed has served as president of the women's ministry for over 20 years. She has been a faithful woman of God in the ministry and is highly admired and respected by all the women in the church. However, recently because of her age and declining health, she has not had the ability to plan some of the events for the ladies, in particular the annual ladies retreat. Overall, the event was successful, but there were several logistical issues that arose largely because Mother Reed forgot to plan for them as she had done in the past. Most of the ladies in the church realize that Mother Reed needs help, but because Mother Reed has done it so well for so long, any offers for help are interpreted as suggesting that she is no longer capable of leading the ministry. Recently, leading up to this year's women's retreat, Pastor appointed an assistant to help her. After a few calls from the recently appointed assistant, inquiring if certain tasks had been completed, Mother Reed refused to work with her, and decided to step down only a few weeks before this year's women's retreat, stating, "It's not right how after all these years they push the old saints to the side for the younger people."

Discussion Questions

(1) Identify the different types of lobsters in the three scenarios.

(2) How should the church handle the various issues presented by the three scenarios?

(3) How well does your church integrate new members, especially those who have special gifts, ministries, and talents, into the church?

(4) Often churches have new member classes to help integrate new members into the ministry but how should the church better prepare existing members, especially ministry leaders, for new members that may join the congregation?

(5) Does your church have any unnecessary written or unwritten rules that hinder new members from participating in ministry?

(6) How should the church respond when it identifies the lobster spirit in its midst towards a new member and their family?

(7) How can a church create a culture and structure that welcomes and easily integrates new members into the church and into various ministries in a church?

(8) How should new members respond when they have been attacked by a lobster spirit in the church?

(9) How can churches prevent those in leadership and service from feeling entitled to a position or threatened to lose their position if someone is sent to help them?

(10) What type of succession planning should a church implement for ministry and auxiliary leaders?

(11) What are some characteristics of a church clique?

(12) How would you know and monitor the reputation of your church as to whether you are warm, friendly, and welcoming, or hostile, cliquish, and unfriendly?

(13) Did Jesus have a clique with the 12 disciples, or with his inner circle of 3?

References

The Church that Cliques
http://www.christianitytoday.com/women-leaders/2015/june/church-that-cliques.html

Why Churches are Unfriendly and Cliquish
https://www.crosswalk.com/blogs/joe-mckeever/why-churches-are-unfriendly-and-cliquish.html

7 of the Most Dangerous Church Cultures
https://www.biblestudytools.com/blogs/ron-edmondson/7-of-the-most-dangerous-church-cultures.html

Are Church Cliques Harmful to Your Spiritual Health?
https://www.charismamag.com/blogs/the-plumb-line/15541-are-church-cliques-harmful-to-your-spiritual-health

Be Guest Friendly
https://churchythoughts.wordpress.com/category/discipleship/

Coping with Cliques
https://www.ucg.org/vertical-thought/coping-with-cliques

Lobster Cannibalism: Crustaceans Starting To Eat Each Other, Probably Because Of Climate Change
https://www.huffingtonpost.com/2013/07/30/lobster-cannibalism_n_3676026.html

10 Weird Facts About Lobsters
https://animals.howstuffworks.com/marine-life/10-weird-facts-lobsters9.htm

Warming seas bring out the cannibal side of our favorite crustaceans.
https://www.motherjones.com/environment/2013/07/climate-change-creating-cannibal-lobsters/

CHAPTER 3

THE OCTOPUS

Over the last 70 years, various studies and surveys have reported that about 40% of Americans attend church on a weekly basis. However, new research has indicated that the number is actually far less. While 40% claim to be regular church attendees, the reality is that less than 20% of Americans attend church on any given Sunday. The Pew Research Center found that only 27% of Millennials attend church on a weekly basis. It is predicted that by 2050, a little over 10% of the population will have attended church on any given Sunday.

Researchers have attempted to identify the cause of this alarming trend. Some blame the recent negative publicity that the church has received from the media. Recent sexual scandals involving pastors and the stereotypes of the rich television preacher making money off of his poor congregation, has caused some to shy away from the church. The change in culture, work schedules, the repeal of blue laws (laws that required certain types of businesses to be closed on Sunday), technology, and competing activities are the culprit. Others have pointed to a biblically-anticipated, overall spiritual decline and diminished importance of God and church attendance in society.

It is understandable that not everyone has the schedule or means to attend every service or event sponsored by the church, nor is church attendance an absolute requirement for spiritual growth. However, further research indicates that many Christians fail to prioritize spending time with God during their own free time. When compared to *hours* spent per week watching television, talking on cellphones, surfing the internet, texting, or playing video games, many Christians spend, at best, only a few *minutes* per week in prayer or bible reading.

So, what does church attendance and personal devotional time have to do with anything? While most of this book has focused on the flaws and failings of the church towards its members, perhaps a culprit responsible for the decline of church attendance, is the most unique cannibalistic animal of them all – the octopus!

It is one thing for an animal to eat its own kind. It is a totally different story for the animal to eat itself. Octopus are known to engage in autophagy — otherwise known as self-eating. Octopi have been observed consuming their own arms, and no one knows why. Biologists once believed that Octopi engaged in a more common practice known as autotomy. In autotomy, the animal will break off a limb as part of a fight, to impress a mate, or to get away from a predator. Other biologists believe that Octopi eat their own arms because of stress, boredom, or a neurological infection in their limbs, similar to Lesch–Nyhan syndrome in humans.

Who are the octopi in the church? Octopi in the church are self-destructive members who do not take advantage of the ministries offered by the church to help them and their families with specific issues they are facing. They are members who never show up to prayer service, Bible study, small group, or special events but often need the most prayer, counseling, and outside attention. A marriage retreat can be planned, but the couple that the pastor has been counseling for the last six months is too busy to attend. The men's ministry can decide to go to a basketball game, but the single-mother who has been crying out for strong male role models for her teenage son forgets about the event. The young adult that has been struggling financially went out of town the last three weekends while the pastor conducted a series on financial literacy. The father that is crying out now because his teenaged daughter is in a state of rebellion was more concerned about her attending every basketball practice and game, but never prioritized bringing his daughter to Sunday school, Vacation Bible School, or to prayer service when she wanted to be involved in church one time before.

The examples can go on and on for any pastor or ministry leader – those who need the ministry the most seem to never be present when an event, conference or bible study, designed with their needs in mind, is held. Generally, in most churches, it is not the faithful, consistent, active attendees that constantly need special prayer or counseling, but often the ones who are inconsistent and routinely absent, for reasons they often <u>CAN</u> control, yet prioritize other things over taking advantage of what is being offered by the church and pastor.

Jesus spoke of it this way in the 4th chapter of the gospel according to Saint Mark, "And these are they who are sown among thorns; such as hear the word, And the cares of this world, and the deceitfulness of riches, and the lusts of other things entering in, choke the word, and it becometh unfruitful." Octopus saints are unable to grow or fight off infection because they do not allow themselves the opportunity to be ministered to or regularly fed the word of God.

The writer of Hebrews goes on to say, not forsaking our meeting together [as believers for worship and instruction], as is the habit of some, but encouraging *one another*, and all the more [faithfully] as you see the day [of Christ's return] approaching." Hebrews 10:25 (AMP). One of the easiest ways for the devil to destroy any believer is through isolation. This is why church, the fellowship of believers on a regular basis, is so vitally important if one wants to be successful in their Christian walk. A student cannot do well in school with poor and irregular attendance. A person cannot become physically fit without regular exercise and eating habits. No team can excel or play at the highest level without practice. While we easily understand this in the natural, the same value is often not given to spiritual matters. While maintaining balance in life is important, it should not come at the expense of one totally neglecting coming to, and serving in, the house of God on a consistent and regular basis. Sadly for my octopus saints "balance" has been substituted for "abandonment" of God's house.

David, understanding this principle, said in Psalms 27:4, "One thing have I desired of the LORD, that will I seek after; that I may dwell in the house of the LORD all the days of my life, to behold the beauty of the LORD, and to enquire in his temple.

It is not suggested that this phenomenon is unique to the church, however it is more prevalent and pervasive. Ask any teacher who is most likely to do an extra credit assignment; it is the high-achieving student. Have a parent-teacher conference, and the parent of the high achieving student is most likely to attend. Ask any community organizer, who is most likely to attend a town hall meeting; it's probably the citizens that are already fully aware and engaged in the neighborhood. Ask any pastor about the member that typically (this is not an absolute) needs less individual counseling; it is likely to be one of the more faithful members.

Is there anything a church can do to change the trend? Jordan Duvall, in an article entitled, "3 Important Church Attendance Statistics & What They Mean For the Modern Church," suggest the following:

1. Not only should a church have a website, but make it interactive to increase direct communication with members and to create a greater sense of community when away from church.
2. Look for progressive ways to reach out to congregants and community members such as using social media, posting sermon notes online, streaming services.

Additional ideas could be the formation of geography-based small cell-group bible studies, conference calls or online bible studies, and the recording & rebroadcasting of services. Church can remain connected to members during the week with group texts, e-mails and online chat-conversations for announcements, prayer requests, and daily devotionals.

Churches should implore creative marketing and advertising for events, while still emphasizing the importance of peer-to-peer invitations. A highly effective form of advertising is to provide opportunities for a variety of past participants to testify about the benefit of an event, service, or teaching series.

Perhaps address an issue of convenience by providing meals before mid-week services, childcare for services geared towards adults-only, or study hall so members can come to church without having to go home, prepare a meal, complete homework, and hopefully, make it back to church on time.

Evaluate who is planning events. It may be important to plan with, rather than merely for target groups. Leaders should periodically evaluate the weekly church schedule/service times to determine if it fits the needs of the present congregation. Periodically survey participants and non-participants to learn how to improve attendance at events. For example, a Friday night youth bible study may have been ideal when the majority of the youth in the church were in elementary or middle school. However, when that same age group reaches high school, with various extracurricular activities such as sports, band competitions, and other social events, a church may have to consider a different day and time for the youth bible study.

Some churches have had the same, exact service schedule since birth without ever considering how it may be impacted by the work schedules or commuting distances of its members. While the church may have been in the same location for decades, the members may no longer live as close to the church. One generation may have lived close enough to walk to the church, but the next generation may live in a different part of town and can't get their as quickly.

Churches may want to consider a zero-based calendar. Under this approach, no special service or event is automatically placed on the calendar for next year unless it can be justified. Some events may only need to have been done once, and only once, or if repeated, perhaps annually, biennially, or on a quadrennial basis. If special events are held too often, then they may become too common and thus, less exciting to attend. Is the attendance increasing each year or decreasing each year? Perhaps it needs to be suspended, revamped, or terminated. If too many events are held, then people will pick-and-choose one over the other. A church may have to prioritize, or create themes for the year, so that members may know what is truly important to attend. If everything is a "mandatory event" or a "must-attend" event, eventually members will no longer be able to make any true distinctions.

Churches must ensure that special events are planned and announced in advance. Too often events are planned at the last minute and members are expected to be there without any advanced notice. Provide members with updated weekly, monthly, and annual church calendars to eliminate the excuse of not knowing an event was scheduled.

Finally, the importance of church attendance and the spiritual benefit of any service or event must be made known to the congregation. Not only must members be reminded of their obligation to be faithful, dutiful members to the church, the era of pastors being able to tell members to show up to church simply because they said so, is likely over. Unless members are made aware of the benefit of attending a particular service or event, they will likely find something else to do or somewhere else to go during that time.

Moreover, church leaders, including the pastor, must be role-models of faithfulness to church. If the pastor is out of his or her pulpit too often, or those in leadership positions are given a "pass" on church attendance, it is likely that other members of the church will follow the same pattern. Don't let it be true when members can say that they don't come to bible study, Sunday evening service, or a special event because they know that the ministry leaders aren't going to be their either.

With prayer, teamwork, and out-of-the box thinking, a church can turn the tide on decreasing church attendance/participation and prevent more members from self-mutilation and destruction found with the Octopus.

Discussion

(1) How can a church better stress the importance, relevancy, and benefit of church membership and regular church attendance?

(2) What type of attendance policies or requirements does your church have for ministry leaders?

(3) Other than guilt, duty, and obligation, what are ways that a church can increase the church attendance of its members?

(4) What innovative ways can the church use technology, small groups, and non-traditional scheduling to accommodate the diverse schedule of church members?

(5) How can the church "bridge-the-gap" when a ministry is created to address a certain need, or a sermon/bible study is designed to address a certain topic, and the ones who could benefit from it the most do not attend, participate, or take advantage of it?

(6) How often do you survey the members of the congregation to learn how to improve church attendance?

(7) How do you determine if a ministry meets too often or not enough to be effective?

(8) How can zero-based scheduling benefit your church?

(9) How do you determine if an event should have only been held once, rotated, or held on a less frequent basis?

(10) How many events in your church are labeled as mandatory or must-attend events?

(11) Are their ways that churches can combine events to leverage finances, attendance, and other resources?

References

3 Important Church Attendance Statistics & What They Mean For The Modern Church

https://stretchinternet.com/church-attendance-statistics-trends-what-they-mean-for-modern-church/

Top 10 reasons people cite for not attending church services
http://www.churchlawandtax.com/web/2010/january/q14.html

Important Church Trends in the Next 10 Years
https://www.christianitytoday.com/edstetzer/2015/april/3-important-trends-in-church-in-next-ten-years.html

7 Startling Facts: An Up Close Look at Church Attendance in America
https://churchleaders.com/pastors/pastor-articles/139575-7-startling-facts-an-up-close-look-at-church-attendance-in-america.html

Zero-Based Church Scheduling
https://thomrainer.com/2017/12/zero-based-church-scheduling/

Octopus Cannibalism Caught on Video for 1st Time
https://www.livescience.com/47982-octopus-cannibalism-video-captured.html

Octopus Cannibalism Captured for First Time
https://www.scientificamerican.com/article/octopus-cannibalism-captured-for-first-time1/

It Turns Out Octopuses Are Occasionally Cannibals, And Here's Why
https://www.thedodo.com/octopus-cannibalism-713614172.html

Do Octopuses Commit Suicide?
https://www.tonmo.com/pages/octopus-suicide/

There May Be A Disease That Makes An Octopus Eat Its Own Arms
https://io9.gizmodo.com/there-may-be-a-disease-that-makes-an-octopus-eat-its-ow-1694165746

CHAPTER 4

THE BULLFROG

Bullfrogs are known to be the predators of the pond. During its lifetime, a bullfrog may eat snakes, scorpions, rodents, birds, crustaceans, worms, and other insects. In addition to their ravenous appetite, bullfrogs also add other bullfrogs to their menu.

Interestingly, bullfrogs do not have any special "weapons" such as claws, fangs, venom, etc. To eat its prey, it uses its large mouth to devour its victims. Bullfrogs hunt by "sitting and waiting," showing only their eyes while the remainder of their body is covered by the water or dirt.

Bullfrogs lie low in wait for prey to cross its path and captures the unsuspecting animal with its quick and powerful tongue. With only a few chomps, the prey is completely devoured and swallowed. At other times, bullfrogs have been known to creep underwater, jump 15-20 feet to shore to capture its prey, and quickly return back to the water to eat it. Showing only their eyes while the remainder of their body is covered by the water or dirt, prey never see the bullfrog coming.

As you have probably predicted, the bullfrogs in the church are those who use their mouths, specifically their tongues, to consume others who live in the pond.

King Solomon writes in Proverbs 18:21, "Death and life are in the power of the tongue, and those who love it will eat its fruit. People have been killed because of slanderous lies told against them."

Apostle James writes in James 3:5-10,

"Likewise, the tongue is a small part of the body, but it makes great boasts. Consider what a great forest is set on fire by a small spark. [6] The tongue also is a fire, a world of evil among the parts of the body. It corrupts the whole body, sets the whole course of one's life on fire, and is itself set on fire by hell.[7] All kinds of animals, birds, reptiles and sea creatures are being tamed and have been tamed by mankind, [8] but no human being can tame the tongue. It is a restless evil, full of deadly poison.[9] With the tongue we praise our Lord and Father, and with it we curse human beings, who have been made in God's likeness. [10] Out of the same mouth come praise and cursing. My brothers and sisters, this should not be"

—(New International Version).

Bullfrogs are those who use their tongues to harm others in the church. Often when people speak of "church hurt", it is likely caused by something hurtful that was said to them. The Bullfrog can manifest itself with insensitive, ill-timed, or inappropriate comments, defamatory and derogatory assertions, critical and condescending remarks, rude and disrespectful e-mail or text messages, or a discouraging or un-affirming statement. Bullfrogs will use the pulpit, restroom, parking lot, pew, social media, testimonial service or even the pastor's office for gossip, slander, and utterly lying on others in the congregation. Equally damaging, can be non-verbal communication transmitted through ill-timed laughter, facial expressions, body language, whispers, and side-bar comments. Coincidentally, the most fatal form of non-verbal communication can be just that, non-verbal—one person refusing to speak to another person in the church.

How often has someone left the church because of hurtful comments from another member? You may know of someone that loved the church and the pastor, were growing spiritually, and was a long time member, but because of a single comment made by a bullfrog, they left their church and, in many cases, church altogether. Bullfrogs make jokes, insensitive comments, condescending remarks, or throw "shade" at other people. Bullfrogs are often meddlesome and busybodies that perpetuate confusion and discord in the church. Bullfrogs will make comments about one's attire, appearance, family, or praise expression—sometimes out of ignorance or habit, but bullfrogs are known for being "messy people" who love confusion. They often put their "foot in their mouth" on a regular basis. Their comments are typically spoken directly to the victim, but more often they are overheard in passing, when they did not think the other person was around and could hear it. Oftentimes, members that know the bullfrog or are "used" to being around them, can often shake it off as "that's just them" or "that's just how they are", but for a guest or a new member, their single inappropriate comment, made at the wrong time or place, can be spiritually fatal to the victim.

First Century BCE Hebrew writer, Ben Sira wrote in Sirach 28:13-26 (GNT)[3] these very relevant and timeless words of wisdom:

"Gossips and liars deserve to be cursed, because they have been the ruin of many people who were minding their own business. Many have had their lives ruined and have been driven from their homes because of people who meddled in their business. Such unwanted interference has resulted in the destruction of strong cities and the homes of respected people. Meddlers have caused faithful wives to be divorced, robbed of everything they had worked for. Anyone who pays attention to slander can never find peace of mind. A whip can raise a welt, but a vicious tongue can break bones. More people have died as a result of loose talk than were ever killed by swords. Count yourself lucky if you have been spared the experience of having irresponsible talk directed against you—if you have never had that iron yoke around your neck or those heavy chains on your legs. Slander leads to a miserable death; but in fact, you'd be better off dead.

Devout people, however, cannot be overcome by slander; they cannot be burned by its flames. Its victims are those who have abandoned the Lord; once the fire of slander has been lit among them, it

---

[3] The Book of **Sirach**, also known as Ecclesiasticus, is part of the Wisdom Literature of the Greek Septuagint and the Latin Vulgate Bible. While originally written in Hebrew, the Book was read only through its Greek translation, known as Σιράχ. The Book was not included in the Hebrew Masoretic Text as part of the Hebrew **Canon** of the Old Testament.

cannot be put out. Slander will pounce on them like a lion and tear them to pieces like a leopard.

Don't you fence in your property? Don't you lock up your money? Well, be just as careful with what you say. Weigh every word, and have a lock ready for your mouth. Someone may be waiting for you to slip, and if you are not careful, you will stumble over your own words and fall down in front of him."

Paul instructs Titus in chapter 3, verses 1 and 2, "Remind the peope… to slander no one, to be peaceable and considerate, and always to be gentle toward everyone" (New International Version).

Apostle Peter lists slander as one of the sins of immature Christians that need to grow up in God. I Peter 2:1-2 says, "Wherefore laying aside all malice, and all guile, and hypocrisies, and envies, and all evil speakings, As newborn babes, desire the sincere milk of the word, that ye may grow thereby:" (King James Version)

In teaching on love to the Corinthian Church, Apostle Paul writes, "Love endures with patience *and* serenity, love is kind *and* thoughtful, and is not jealous *or* envious; love does not brag and is not proud *or* arrogant. It is not rude; it is not self-seeking, it is not provoked [nor overly sensitive and easily angered]; it does not take into account a wrong *endured*. It does not rejoice at injustice, but rejoices with the truth [when right and truth prevail]. Love bears all things [regardless of what comes], believes all things [looking for the best in each one], hopes all things [remaining steadfast during difficult times], endures all things [without weakening]" (1 Corinthians 13:4-7, Amplified Bible).

Apostle Paul speaks of busybodies deriving from idleness. 2 Thessalonians 3:11-12 says, "We hear that some among you are idle and disruptive. They are not busy; they are busybodies. Such people we command and urge in the Lord Jesus Christ to settle down and earn the food they eat" (New International Version). Paul reiterates this point in I Timothy 5:13, Besides, they get into the habit of being idle and going about from house to house. And not only do they become idlers, but also busybodies who talk nonsense, saying things they ought not to" (New International Version).

People tend to concern themselves with the affairs of others when they seemingly have no business of their own that they should be attending. This is not always the case. However, often the person who is sweeping around someone else's door needs to go home and clean their house! To put another way: before an individual gets a warrant to search someone else's closet for skeletons, chances are they need to deal with the bones in their backyard, first. One can go on and on, but one more, cliché "people who live in glass houses shouldn't throw stones."

Bullfrogs may use their tongues to eat but their appetite is derived from what is called a critical spirit. Dale A. Robbins, in her article entitled, "Do You Have a Critical Spirit", defines a critical spirit as "an obsessive attitude of criticism and fault-finding, which seeks to tear others down — not the same thing as what is sometimes called 'constructive criticism'". While other versions use the word "judge" the Amplified Version translates the word in Romans14:13 as "criticize." Paul writes, "Then let us not criticize one another anymore, but rather determine this—not to put an obstacle or a stumbling block *or* a source of temptation in another believer's way.

John Ankerberg Show, in his article, "How to Understand and Approach Someone With a Critical Spirit", provides the following 10 reasons for a critical spirit: sinful or selfish nature, poor self-concept, little or no grace, pessimism or negativity, insecurity, immaturity, unrenewed mind, a root of bitterness, bad company, and the devil.

Both Show and Robbins agree, "The only criticism that is ever constructive is that which is expressed in love to 'build up', not to tear down — it is always expressed face-to-face, never behind their back."

As with bullfrogs, there are those who will lay low and do nothing in the church but will be the first to use their tongue to critique and complain. They will come out of hiding just to cause confusion and dissention in the church. There are some people that have absolutely nothing positive to say about anyone or anything in the church. They will criticize the praise team, but won't sing, criticize the preacher, but won't pray for him, talk about what the church "ain't got", but won't give a dime to make it happen. Bullfrogs will come to the church meeting and not give any input, but will stay in the parking lot for an hour after the meeting to give their insight on what was discussed during the meeting. Bullfrogs are like Monday morning sports commentators after the Sunday football game. Sports commentators will review and discuss every play of the game, both good and bad. Similarly, bullfrogs, will call several of their friends, both inside and outside the church, to analyze and discuss every aspect of the worship service from start to finish.

In addition, bullfrogs will often go out of their way to find an audience. Someone with a bullfrog spirit will call, visit, or inbox a member to "check on them" while their true motive is to gossip, slander, complain, and critique other frogs in the pond. Anything and anyone who comes in or near the pond is subject to consumption by the bullfrog. The pastor, pastor's spouse, pastor's children, young people—it doesn't matter. If the bullfrog can put its tongue on it and get its mouth around it, then it is going to try to devour it.

To address this issue, a church may have to undergo sensitivity training and have bible studies on controlling the tongue, effective communication and listen skills, and bible-based conflict resolution that deal with real comments and scenarios. Authors such as Show, Robbins, and others enumerate on several specific, practical, biblical ways to differentiate between constructive criticism and critical spirits, how to cure critical spirits, and how to offer constructive feedback.

Author Lori Hatcher in her article, "Five Ways to Overcome a Critical Spirit" gives biblical and practical advice to help church bullfrogs overcome their critical spirits. Merely speaking in generalities is likely insufficient. A teaching on the poisonous tongue requires providing definitions on such words as gossip, slander, backbiting, and reviling. For years, these terms are repeated in our churches, but we have never examined their definitions or thought about different ways that people engage in them. Effective teaching on the harm a deadly tongue can inflict will likely require the teacher to provide students with specific examples, scenarios, vignettes, or illustrations of harmful statements. Perhaps you could utilize the help of the church drama ministry to provide examples of harmful speech. Ironically, because many are programed to be critical and to see the flaws in others, it will be easy for the class to dissect the scenarios presented and learn from them.

While many intentionally make derogatory comments, some people honestly do not know the implications of their statements and how it can impact others. Not until many have participated in an open discussion or role-played with hypothetical or real-life scenarios consisting of harmful and hurtful comments and gestures, it will never resonate in their minds. Conversations about the what-when-where-why-and-how a statement is made can be tremendously beneficial to a church. Have the congregation ask whether a statement or comment was appropriate, if the situation could have been handled better, or if the response was appropriate and perfectly acceptable. In many cases, people just don't think before they speak. Give them something to think about and perhaps a church can reduce the number of bullfrogs in the congregation.

Likewise, realizing that all of us are flawed individuals, constantly in the need of God's grace, and prone to putting our "foot in our mouth", it is important that when offended, we should go directly to the person who offended us, without assuming the worse, but giving the other person the benefit of the doubt and an opportunity to explain themselves. Whether they apologize or not, we are required to forgive. If an apology is given and reconciliation is possible, we should try to repair and restore our relationship with our brother or sister in Christ.

Members must be made more aware of the potential impact of their communications on others, but members must be taught how to confront a bullfrog and put an end to the cannibalism in the church. Who can forget the infamous line from Mrs. Jenkins from the 90's hit sketch comedy show *In Living Color,* "I ain't one to gossip, so you ain't heard that from me!" Too often, church members fall into the fallacy that as long as they did not share the slander or repeat the gossip, that it is acceptable for them to listen to it. People like being in the know, getting the inside scoop, and hearing the latest news. In many ways, the one who consumes garbage is worse than the one who shares the garbage. One of the best ways to keep a bullfrog in the church is by provide it with the next lily pad to leap onto in the pond. As long as a bullfrog has an eager audience for gossip or criticism, it will continue its activity, unabated. While one may not have robbed the bank, they are criminally liable for driving the get-away car. Similarly, it's impossible for a person to share gossip, slander, or criticism without an eager and enthusiastic audience. Don't be the lily pad that the bullfrog lands on next!

Bryant Evans in his article, "Stop Gossip in the Church" writes, "Gossip is particularly damaging in the local church because people are often more open with fellow Christians about their weaknesses and needs. And because those weaknesses are out in the open it may be that gossip is more common in the church than anywhere else." Evans provides five steps to stop a gossiping tongue:

1. Make a conscious effort to monitor your own words.
2. Make a conscious effort to monitor your own hearing.
3. Speak out to stop gossip.
4. Assume unflattering stories are false.
5. Let gossip end with you.

Before this chapter is concluded, it must be stated that not all stern rebuke or word of correction are inappropriate or harmful speech. Admonition, done in love, may in fact sting or even hurt, but is often necessary for spiritual growth and development. We often are more receptive to a teacher, doctor, coach, or personal trainer telling us the truth than our pastor or other leader in the congregation. Paul instructed Timothy to reprove (reprimand or censure), rebuke (express sharp disapproval or criticism) and exhort (strongly encourage or urge), but with longsuffering (patience) and doctrine (teaching). Those who God has placed in our lives have the right and responsibility to confront us in love, and by the leading of the Holy Spirit, if we are out of line, falling into sin, failing to perform our duties, or to resolve a difficult matter in the church. In this regard, those in spiritual leadership are not acting as cannibalistic bullfrogs but as loving shepherds.

In closing, never forget that the goal of the enemy is to steal, kill, and to destroy. He is also referred to as "the prince of the air". Hence, the devil has a way of corrupting communication such that what is spoken and what is heard may be totally different. He will use words, actions, and misdeeds to remove us from the place where God wants us. This trick of the enemy must be exposed and eliminated. While there are toxic ponds and bullfrogs in every church, we should never allow one off-hand comment by an individual to totally uproot us from where God has planted us. Sometimes genuine people can make incorrect assumptions, inappropriate comments, hurtful statements, and tell bad jokes without knowing it. Give them a chance to know about it, learn from it, and seek forgiveness for it. Recognize it for what it is - a tactic of the devil intended to kill us spiritually. Thus, my words to you as were Paul's in Thessalonians are, "But ye, brethren, be not weary in well doing" (2 Thessalonians 3:13, King James Version). Let the lions roar, the dogs bark, and the bullfrogs croak. In the end the most important voice we all want to hear is God saying to us, "Well done thy good and faithful servant."

Discussion Questions

(1) How do you distinguish between a person who provides helpful and insightful constructive feedback and a person with a destructive and divisive critical spirit?

(2) How can a church provide members with an opportunity to express concerns or share ideas in a constructive environment?

(3) When is it appropriate to leave a church because of something that someone said to them?

(4) What is the proper way to handle gossip, slander, untrue statements or false allegation?

(5) What is the appropriate way to reprove or rebuke someone?

(6) How should a church deal with a bullfrog once they have been identified?

(7) What is the difference between gossip and the sharing of important information that leadership should be made aware?

(8) How can you teach members to be more sensitive to both verbal and nonverbal comments?

(9) How should a situation be resolved when two members are not speaking to each other?

(10) Is it possible for a bullfrog or person with a critical spirit to be transformed?

(11) How can the church help heal someone who has experienced church hurt because of a bullfrog in the congregation?

References

Insensitive Christians: Learn to Reflect the Heart of Christ
http://www.heavenlymanna.net/christianArticle.php?article_id=998

Slander, Gossip, and Evil Speech: the Bible Teaching
http://www.gospelway.com/morality/slander.php

Gossip in the Church
https://www.crosswalk.com/church/pastors-or-leadership/gossip-in-the-church-505728.html

Stop Gossip in the Church
http://preachersstudyblog.com/2010/04/stop-gossip-in-the-church/

Do you have a Critical Spirit?
http://www.victorious.org/pub/critical-spirit-106

How to Understand and Approach Someone with a Critical Spirit
https://www.jashow.org/articles/christian-living/godly-living/understand-approach-someone-critical-spirit/

Confronting Sin Versus a Critical Spirit
http://www.christianitytoday.com/biblestudies/bible-answers/personalconcerns/confrontingsin.html

5 Ways to Overcome a Critical Spirit
https://www.crosswalk.com/faith/women/5-ways-to-overcome-a-critical-spirit.html

Invading Bullfrogs Appear Nearly Unstoppable
https://news.nationalgeographic.com/news/2004/09/0928_040928_bullfrog_2.html

Kermit the Cannibal? Frogs Sometimes Eat Each Other
https://www.livescience.com/52086-frog-cannibalism-study.html

American Bullfrogs
http://www.biokids.umich.edu/critters/Lithobates_catesbeianus/

CHAPTER 5

THE SAND TIGER SHARK

Sand tiger sharks, also known as sand sharks, sand tigers, or gray nurse sharks, have sharp teeth that protrude in all directions, even when they shut their mouths. Despite their fearsome name and appearance, they are known to attack humans only when provoked. Because of their relatively peaceful nature, sand tigers are the most common sharks found in public aquariums.

Mother tiger sharks are unique in several ways. First, during early embryotic development, a female sand tiger shark may have as many as 50 embryos in her two uteruses. Secondly, tiger sharks have a long gestation period of twelve months. Because a tiger shark has two uteruses and a lengthy gestation period, a mother tiger shark can actually mate with two different tiger sharks and carry the fertilized eggs of both partners in her womb. Most sharks give birth to multiple babies at once. However, the sand tiger sharks can only give birth to two babies at a time — one from each of their two uteri.

The question is then asked,

what happened to the other 50 or more fertilized eggs if only two "pups" are actually born? Did the mother shark miscarry? Did the unborn sharks die because of a lack of nutrition or over-crowding?

A Stony Brook marine biologist, Demian Chapman, sought answers to this very question. Since the 1980's, Chapman observed pregnant tiger sharks and found embryos in the stomach of other embryos. "This in utero cannibalism, taking place about five months into the gestation, allows the remaining embryo to feed itself on its siblings' bodies and the mother's nutrient supply."

To further his research, from 2008 to 2012, Chapman observed 15 pregnant tiger sharks in various stages of pregnancy to determine the paternity of the surviving pups. Sharks in the early stage had more fertilized eggs in the uterus, whereas those in the final stage of pregnancy only had one egg per uterus. DNA testing revealed that the tiger shark mated more than once and that the two sharks that survived were from the same father.

"In one of nature's most extreme cases of sibling rivalry, the sand tiger shark (Carcharias taurus) is the only shark on Earth that devours its younger brothers and sisters while still in the womb." While there is no proven explanation for embryonic cannibalism, clearly, it is the "ultimate survival of the fittest". Some have suggested that it is merely the older and larger sharks devouring their siblings because of space and nutrients. Others have suggested that it is mere competition with the larger, stronger, and more aggressive sharks, not necessarily, the oldest that make it to birth.

The third common theory is that of sexual selection. Simply put, under sexual selection, the female picks the best partner to mate. However, because of the aggressive nature of tiger sharks, it is believed that the first mate may not have been the "preferred" or "selected" mate. Therefore, the female tiger shark will mate a second time, perhaps more, while pregnant, to find her "preferred" partner, or the "competitively superior male."

While research has been unable to track which male's offspring survived to be birthed in all 15 cases, the offspring were full siblings. Evidence also suggests that the "best set" of embryos actually survive. "The researchers' tests suggest that sexual competition among male sand tigers continues well after the sperm has fertilized the egg — their sons and daughters are left to fight it out, too." This outcome suggests that embryonic cannibalism helped eliminate other fathers' offspring.

What is the comparison of the tiger shark to the church? If one considers the ratio of both unfertilized eggs and fertilized eggs in the mother tiger shark to the number of offspring birthed, we find that the tiger shark represents the church with a conversion and retention issue, also known as the "backdoor problem".

Author Rob Overton describes the backdoor problem as,

"people who made an initial connection, assimilated into one of the main areas of emphasis in the church and made church a part of their normal routine. I am not talking about people who have never connected into the life of the church. If a person never successfully connects, then they just turn around and go out the

same way they came in, through the front door. Initial visitor connection requires its own proactive process and has a different set of dynamics."

A tiger shark church is able to attract many visitors, with a significant number of them actually joining the church and becoming actively engaged and participating in ministry. But after a short period of time, the individuals and families leave the ministry, not to join another church, but most often to leave church altogether. In like manner, the mother tiger shark may have dozens of unfertilized and fertilized eggs in her womb, but is only able to give birth to two of them. If your church constantly laments about how large your church membership would be today if it had retained a certain percentage of those who, not just visited, but were actually baptized or joined the church, then perhaps you have a retention issue, commonly referred to as a "backdoor problem".

Different from the "front door problem", which is described as an issue of evangelism and attracting people to a church, the "backdoor problem" is a metaphor referring to the process of people quietly leaving a church after a period of time. While it is one issue for a guest to a visit a church and not return—what makes members of a church turn around and leave church? Just as scientists went through great lengths to observe and study tiger sharks over a period of time to determine the cause, similarly church leaders must observe, test, dissect, and even run a DNA test to determine why people leave or stay, and what the common path or pattern is before someone exits out the back door.

Many churches do very little to understand the issue of retention. Some just dismiss it as a normal course of business. While it is true that many will leave a church for various reasons, it is important to understand those reasons, and when possible, make corrections. Too many churches take the parable of the sower too literally. Just because Jesus said, "some seed fell on stony ground, some fell by the wayside, some fell among thorns, and others fell on good ground" – does not necessarily mean that one out of four people who join your church will automatically leave. The reality is that the seed which fell on good ground actually produced a 30, 60, 100 fold harvest. If the seed that fell on good ground can produce exponentially, then we do not have a simple one out of four retention rate.

Furthermore, the farmer should be asking himself if it is possible to do a better job of protecting his seed and bringing it to harvest. While it may be impossible to protect every seed, can we reduce the number that is devoured by birds, choked by the weeds, or fails to take root? If the farmer fails to ask himself these questions on a regular basis and implement new strategies to produce a greater yield, he will ultimately have the same results.

Many churches have a "red carpet" approach to evangelism. Churches spend a great deal of time, money, and training to invite people to church, witness to the lost, help them to give their life to Christ, and then join a particular church. Churches can be very visitor sensitive, overtly friendly, and have powerful worship services to attract people, but have absolutely nothing in place to support or retain people once they join or give their life to Christ. A good hospital must not only have a delivery room, but also a nursery to care for the newborn baby. The church cannot grow or survive if its culture is that of the tiger shark womb, "survival of the fittest." Alternatively, church culture must be an incubator designed for success.

Many churches know how to court a person with nice gifts, dinners, and dates, or recruit, like a college for example, with awesome tours, festivities, and scholarships. Once they have won the heart of their target, or the student officially enrolls, they are cast aside as merely one in the number. If a church can identify the location of the back door and who is mostly likely to exit through it, the church can then formulate a strategy to address the issues. If there are common themes attributing to why people leave our church(es), then perhaps we should be less thin skinned and defensive to find out if there is something we can do about it.

Like any business, a church may have to ask itself tough, searing questions to get the answers it needs. Is it a question of doctrine or is it the lack of a new member class to address doctrinal questions in a safe environment? Is it a matter of assimilation, or fitting-in, but the church has no program or initiative to intentionally integrate new members into the church family?

Are old friends and old habits pulling the person back out of the church because the church has not created a mentorship or discipleship program to help those navigate their earlier stages of their Christian walk? Are there too many cliques in the church and too few opportunities to serve in the church? Does work, travel, sickness, or discouragement cause a person to miss a few

Sundays, and because no one noticed or reached out to the person, they now feel unwanted, unwelcomed, and unloved? Are those in leadership too insensitive, invisible, and inaccessible? Similar to the hit TV show, "Undercover Boss", church leadership may have to put itself in the position of a visitor or a new member to truly understand their issues and experiences with the church.

While it is true that all energy cannot be focused on retention, and as some see it, "chasing after people", we must never forget the parable of Jesus regarding the shepherd who left the 99 to go after the one. There are times when God requires us to direct our attention and focus to go after the one. Church hurt is real. Sadly, for many people, joining church has been the most disappointing, devastating, and damaging experience in their lives. If left untreated, the person may suffer from irreparable harm and perhaps spiritual death.

However, the eye on the back door cannot, nor should it, be managed solely by the pastor. It is an unrealistic expectation of the pastor to notice and contact everyone who missed service on any given Sunday. However, if the culture of the entire church is one that notices and contacts people, thus, making the pastor's job easier, then the responsibility of retention is on the entire congregation and not just one person. Moreover, it must be the culture of the church to simply love and care about each other. It is one thing to reach out to someone out of duty or obligation versus someone who reaches out because they are spirit-led and genuinely concerned about the individual.

In Ecclesiastes 4:12, the bible speaks of a three-fold cord that is not easily broken. For a person to remain connected to a church, the relationship must go beyond that person and the pastor, or the person who initially invited them to church; a third strand who will help keep the person connected to the ministry must also be a part. Too many members are falling through the cracks because there are too many holes in the nest. In many cases, it will be too late to recover those who fell through the cracks, but if a church can locate the hole and repair it in time, hopefully, it can prevent others from falling through.

To prevent the tiger shark culture from being the culture of your church, it is important to learn who is heading for the door, how to guard the door, and how to close the door.

A. Who's heading for the backdoor?

Who is likely to leave a church? Have people become less involved in ministry or never became involved? Is it because they never had an opportunity or had a bad experience with the opportunity? Are there personal or familial issues that might discourage them from coming to church? Has the individual's enthusiasm towards church noticeably changed? Do they seem disconnected, withdrawn, or uninterested? It may be that their worship has changed, their giving has changed, and their overall demeanor during service is different. Perhaps they no longer bring guests with them to church or when they come, it's more common for them to arrive late or leave early. Has the individual expressed a question or concern that has not been addressed properly (if at all)? While it is true, that many unique experiences – marriage, job, etc., come with a honeymoon period, the church should not become a nightmare experience. In some cases, to learn who is heading for the door, it is as simple as observing the fact that the person who once sat near the front is now sitting in the back of the church near the door!

B. How do we guard the door?

When we guard the door, we are not saying that we should bolt it and block it. For some, it is better for them to leave than to stay and destroy a ministry. However, a church should take reasonable steps to prevent God-sent people from leaving because of our own negligence or malfeasance. Four things a church should utilize to help guard the door: (1) measure; (2) monitor; (3) mechanisms, and (4) ministry.

MEASURE

It is important for churches to measure not only weekly attendance, but also involvement, participation, and satisfaction. While attendance may show a pattern or trend for the entire church, it often does not show individual or family attendance. Most churches merely conduct a headcount and not an actual roll call. Attendance may need to be taken during Sunday School, Small Group, Bible Study, Youth Group, Special Events, and practices. Additionally, church may need to conduct periodic ministry fairs, involvement inventories, and satisfaction surveys to help get members involved or to learn more about issues they may have with the church.

MONITOR

Data collected is of no benefit if it is not reported and analyzed. If a small group leader or Sunday school teacher notices that certain ones are absent, or behavior suggests something is wrong, to whom is it reported? Ministries have to be careful that this meeting on attendance does not become a time of gossip or assumptions, yet at the same time, once we are aware, it should produce a correct and corresponding action to address it.

MECHANISMS

Does the church have an established protocol to address complaints, dissatisfaction, disengagement, absenteeism, or behavior that suggests a person is discouraged or in need of assistance? After how many unannounced or unexcused absences can happen before a member receives a phone call? Even if considered inactive, are there times during special events or services where the church will reach out again to those who have stopped coming to church?

MINISTER

Once we have measured, monitored, and mechanized our backdoor strategy, the final prong is the minister. Who will make the visits, the phone calls, send the inbox or text messages to reach out? As stated earlier, this cannot be a one-person operation, but it requires the attention of many. Additionally, not everyone is uniquely suited for a rescue and recovery mission within a church. Only people with the unique gifts of the spirit, confidentiality, and the heart of the church and pastor, can work in this special operations ministry. However, just as Jethro instructed Moses, God will give the pastor people with his heart and spirit that will aid in the retention of members in the church family.

C. How do we close the door?

Various authors have written on the subject of retention, and in their books, they address the following: (1) expectation, (2) groups, (3) involvement, (4) relationships, and (5) incorporation.

- **Expectations:** Make membership meaningful. In many organizations, standards and requirements have been lowered to make it easy or less burdensome. However, research indicates that people will often treat something that has less standards with less regard than something with high standards. People seek the most prestigious universities, professional organizations, and athletic programs because they want high standards and accountability. Lowering the bar in hopes that more will enter is often the easy way for people to find the exit. What are your expectations as it relates to attendance, giving, service, evangelism, and Christian living? Does your church have a standard or even a job description for the duties and responsibilities for new members? Do people who have never been associated with a church or religion know what is expected of them? While we do not want to scare them away with rules, regulations, doctrine books, discipline manuals, or contracts, but we can't blame people for being poor members if they do not know "why" certain things are beneficial to them.

- **Groups:** It is important that both large and small churches have established groups and ministries to serve the members in the congregation. While some ministries are fairly standard with most churches—men, women, and youth—each church should focus on the unique needs as well as resources of the congregation. Whether the ministries are based on age, gender, profession, background (both positive and negative experiences), geography, hobbies, marital status or some type of need, it is important to link new members to others who are relatable and those who are uniquely equipped to help them in prayer, encouragement, mentorship and overall Christian development.

- **Involvement:** When related to small groups, involvement is less focused on the needs of the member, but rather on the gifts they can offer to the ministry. While everyone is not gifted in the same area, it is important to get people involved, working, serving, and sharing their gifts and talents as soon as possible. The more people are vested, connected, utilized, needed, and appreciated, the better. Most people seek not just to be served, but desire an opportunity to serve. People will leave to go where they are wanted, needed, and appreciated. Through serving, we often foster and cultivate our callings and gifts while developing relationships with others. Rather than wait for the new member to volunteer, ministry and auxiliary leaders should be trained to identify, recruit, and train new members for ministry opportunities. Similarly, through new member classes, spiritual gift assessments, ministry fairs and involvement inventories, if the information is not just merely collected, but shared with relevant parties, then hopefully new members can find their niche in the ministry.

- **Relationships**: Existing relationships must be strengthened, and new relationships must be established. Beyond small groups and ministry involvement, churches must provide members with the opportunity to fellowship and get to know each other outside of a worship service. If a person only comes and sits with those who they know for 90 minutes, once a week, a year from now, they will only know those same people and those that sit in their section of the church. Churches must develop intentional activities, not just for new members to get to know each other, but also to meet the more established members of the church.

Likewise, it is important for existing, or long term members, to be taught and reminded that much of the work of assimilating new members into the family, is not the responsibility of the new members, but of the existing members. In a family, when a new baby is born or adopted, they know absolutely nothing of the history, traditions, culture or practices of said family. It is the responsibility of the parents, siblings, and extended family members to assimilate and incorporate that baby into the family.

Similarly, the whole church must have a culture of befriending and integrating new members into the church family. While church cliques will be dealt with in another chapter, members must be made aware of the importance of not just remaining in their after-church huddles with their friends and loved ones, while the new family leaves, both literally and figuratively, out the back door of the church. If a church really has embraced the culture of family, it will extend beyond the time and location for church, but members will call, text, e-mail and inbox each other, as led by the spirit throughout the week, to strengthen the bonds of the church family.

Discussion Questions

(1) In what manner does your church track church as well as monitor individual attendance, participation, and overall satisfaction?

(2) What are some clues that a person might be headed for the back door?

(3) Describe the process your church has in place to identify and reach out to people who are absent from church?

(4) What are the top reasons former member give for leaving your church and/or not returning to your church?

(5) Is there anything that could be done to improve your church retention rate?

(6) How do you know when it is in the best interest of everyone for an individual or family to leave a church?

(7) Which special events or occasions does your church uses to reconnect with former members?

(8) When and where are the requirements and expectations of new members communicated to them?

(9) What percentage of first-time visitors have visited a second or more time? What percentage have actually join the church? What percentage are activity involved in 1 or more ministries? What percentage of members have been there 1, 5, 10, 20 or more? Do you know why they actually stayed?

(10) How can a church develop a culture that everyone is responsible for evangelism, assimilation, and retention of new members?

References

Another look at the back door
https://www.ministrymagazine.org/archive/2009/10/another-look-at-the-back-door

Effective new members' retention strategy must go beyond programs
https://news.adventist.org/en/all-commentaries/commentary/go/-/effective-new-members-retention-strategy-must-go-beyond-programs/

Four Principles for Membership Retention
http://www.christianitytoday.com/pastors/2007/july-online-only/thom-rainer-four-principles-membership-retention.html

4 Ways Churches Can Close the Back Door
https://churchleaders.com/outreach-missions/outreach-missions-how-tos/139399-the-big-4-closing-the-back-door.html

Attendance and the Back Door
http://www.churchlead.com/home/view/1503/attendance_
and_the_back_door

Top 7 Ways to Close the Back Door of Your Church
http://www.churchlead.com/home/view/1599/top_7_ways_
to_close_the_back_door_of_your_church

For sand tiger sharks, a deadly, cannibalistic battle inside the womb is part of evolution
https://www.washingtonpost.com/national/health-science/
for-sand-tiger-sharks-a-deadly-cannibalistic-battle-inside-
the-womb-is-part-of-evolution/2013/04/30/2b14dbbc-
b1bf-11e2-bbf2-a6f9e9d79e19_story.html?utm_
term=.0b279cfa2db8

'Cannibal' Shark Eats Its Siblings In The Womb
http://www.businessinsider.com/cannibal-sand-tiger-shark-
eats-siblings-2013-4

Biology of Sharks and Rays
http://www.elasmo-research.org/education/topics/lh_
intrauterine_cannibalism.htm

Cannibalistic Baby Sharks
https://www.discovery.com/tv-shows/shark-week/videos/
cannibalistic-baby-sharks

Cannibal sharks eat siblings in utero
http://www.cbc.ca/news/technology/cannibal-sharks-eat-
siblings-in-utero-1.1383868

Scientists unravel mystery of cannibal shark embryos
By Mai Ngọc Châu, Contributor MAY 1, 2013

https://www.csmonitor.com/Science/2013/0501/Scientists-
unravel-mystery-of-cannibal-shark-embryos

CHAPTER 6

THE POLAR BEAR

Visualize traveling by ship through the picturesque and pristine arctic. Everything is fresh and clean. The water is pure and shines like crystal. The snow glistens with freshness. There is peace and tranquility. Nature, at its best! Quiet, calm, unpolluted, and untainted: an escape, a refuge from modern technology, the noises of urban life, and the hustle and bustle of everyday living. It is here, in the arctic, that one perhaps finds himself not only closer to nature, but closer to God.

From this vantage point, one sees on the horizon two polar bears, one large and one small running across the snow. How cute and cuddly – a postcard in the making! A male bear and its cub out on a morning stroll to catch fish for breakfast. However, upon further observation you notice that the two bears are not running together, but in fact the larger male bear is chasing the smaller cub. You immediately think how humorous it is to see a father chasing a runaway toddler. You eventually see the bear catch up to the cub and grab it by the neck, as if to routinely return the cub back to its den. This time, however, it is different. You begin to see red on the pure white snow.

Oh no, you think, perhaps the father bear bit too hard or the cub made an abrupt move to cause the bleeding. Then, as you continue to observe intently, it happens. You realize too late that the male bear is not there to save the cub, but to cannibalize it. Horror and fear now take over as you realize what you just witnessed. How could this be, in such a picturesque and pristine place? A place that now has been contaminated by the bright red trail of smeared blood across the pure white snow.

Questions emerge—was this an accident? Is this a common occurrence? Is there a reasonable explanation? How could such a violent act occur in such a peaceful place by seemingly such cute and cuddly animals? Can the trend be reversed? Some scholars believe that this is a new trend caused by global warming, the melting arctic, and shortage of food; others argue that the phenomenon is common, but only recently been observed.

This chapter will speak to one of the taboo subjects in the church: sexual abuse and misconduct by church leadership. In recent years, numerous allegations of sexual misconduct have hit the headlines often involving priests and the Catholic Church. The storyline is often the same: numerous children, mostly boys, who were the victims of molestation and pedophilia by their local priests. Churches, rather than go public, decided to reassign priests to new churches, only to see the same behavior repeated elsewhere, with a different group of children.

The reality is that the issues of sexual abuse, incest, molestation, pedophilia, sexual harassment, sexual assault, rape and infidelity are not a Catholic Church problem; it is an issue that all churches and denominations must confront and handle properly. A 2008 article, by Christianity Today, reported, "Verdicts, judgments, or settlements exceeding hundreds of millions of dollars have been levied against Protestant churches for sexual abuse allegations arising from children participating in ministry programs."

This issue is not limited to sexual abuse and molestation of children, but also to sexual assault and harassment of adults. Alarming are the findings of a 2008 survey reported in the Christian Post stating, "More than a quarter of Christian women have experienced sexual harassment and of those, one fourth said it happened in a church or ministry setting, a new study shows." Ranging from inappropriate conversations and suggestive jokes to unauthorized touching and actual rape, many women have faced the same hostile work environments in the church as others have experiences at their secular jobs. Further, nearly half of the women surveyed stated that they did not report the harassment to anyone.

The issue of sexual misconduct is not limited to the priest or the pastor, but can occur at all levels of leadership, and at any activity in the church. While it may not make the evening news, the more common forms of sexual misconduct can happen with others, in less obvious staff members: youth leader, choir director, van driver, Sunday school teacher, and administrative staff. A 1996 study in Hammar's *Church Law and Tax Report* found that half of all sexual misconduct offences in churches were committed by volunteer workers.

In addition to staff members, sexual misconduct can be caused by members, or non-members, during authorized church activities or on member's personal time. Because of the welcoming, trusting, and open nature of church congregations, they often become a prime target of predators.

Making this problem worse is the addition of what is referred to as peer-to-peer abuse, or abuse by children to other children. The same Christianity Today article reports, "Criminal prosecutors report nearly 300 percent increase in reports of peer-to-peer abuse in the past five years."

Regardless of who does it and where it is done, sexual misconduct in the church, like the cannibalistic polar bear, creates a bright red trail of smeared blood across the pure white snow. For various reasons, generally speaking, the church has mishandled the issue of sexual abuse and assault. Maureen Farrell Garcia, in her article entitled, "How to Spot Sexual Abuse in Your Church Understanding the Dynamics of Sexual Abuse is the First Step" writes that the problem is that the church has various misconceptions about sexual abuse. For example, she states that, "becoming Christian, or truly repenting and being forgiven heals the sex offender." She elaborates on the point by saying, "Sexual offending cannot be addressed as just a terrible "sin" that is fixed instantly through forgiveness... Recovery requires commitment, effort, and time that hopefully results in emotional and spiritual health and maturity." Secondly, she expounded upon the notion that everyone should be forgiven and accepted in the church family. While it is true that sex offenders are sinners in need of saving grace and can be forgiven of their sins and transformed in their minds, a church must not prematurely, if ever, let down its guard when it comes to a known sex offender in the congregation. Thirdly, Garcia writes, another misconception is the idea that sex abuse is merely sinful sex, as opposed to abuse within a sexual context. She further writes, "Even though we label this abuse 'sexual,' it is not merely sexual, since it includes other types of abuse such as emotional, psychological, and spiritual abuse as well." Garcia concludes her article by listing four common traits of sex offenders to help church identify known, as well as unknown, sexual predators in the congregation.

One wonders if the church is merely ignorant, naive, or ambivalent to sexual abuse, or if the problem is an issue of the church trying to preserve its reputation at the expense of protecting its most vulnerable members. In recent news, the hashtag "#MeToo" has been popularized as women have shared their various experiences of sexual harassment in the workplace. Perhaps lesser known, but equally important is the hashtag movement "#ChurchToo", as numerous individuals have described their experience with sexual assault or abuse in the church. In many cases, the horrible pattern is similar—young girl is assaulted by an older man, perhaps a youth minister or pastor, but when the young lady comes forward, she is accused of lying or blamed for the incident. Occasionally, the predator, at most, was given a slap on the wrist, forgiven, and allowed to remain in their position. Several lamented at how the church celebrated the confession and forgiveness of the predator while shaming, shunning, and ridiculing the actual victims.

Gregory Love and Kimberlee Norris in their article entitled, "Sexual Abuse Issues in the Church; Raising the Bar" lists five misconceptions churches have as it relates to protecting itself and members from sexual abuse and assault. The article addresses such misconceptions as: (1) churches assuming that child sexual abuse will not occur within its congregation; (2) over reliance on criminal background checks of staff to protect children; (3) church policies that are poorly crafted, unknown and not enforced by staff; (4) over-reliance on child-tag and surveillance systems to protect kids; and (5) churches believing that it can't afford effective safety systems. The worse thing a church can do is put its head in the sand, like an ostrich, ignore the problem and hope that it will take care of itself.

While many have written on the topic of sexual abuse and assault in the church, identifying the causes as well as providing possible solutions to mitigate the problem, it is important that we also examine the Word of God for guidance in such matters. Although the words "sexual assault" is not mentioned in the Bible, there are numerous instances of rape and infidelity in the scriptures. Let's briefly examine a few.

TAMAR

2 Samuel 13:19-22 (New International Version) records the rape of King David's daughter, Tamar, by her half-brother Amnon.

19 Tamar put ashes on her head and tore the ornate robe she was wearing. She put her hands on her head and went away, weeping aloud as she went.

20 Her brother Absalom said to her, "Has that Amnon, your brother, been with you? Be quiet for now, my sister; he is your brother. Don't take this thing to heart." And Tamar lived in her brother Absalom's house, a desolate woman.

21 When King David heard all this, he was furious. 22 And Absalom never said a word to Amnon, either good or bad; he hated Amnon because he had disgraced his sister Tamar.

There are three points to glean from David's total mishandling of the situation. First, the sad reality is that sexual abuse is most often inflicted by someone the victim knows and trust, specifically, a family member or close family friend. Here, it was not a stranger who raped Tamar, but her half-brother. Secondly, while the scripture says that David was angry about the situation regarding Tamar, he did absolutely nothing about the situation. David did not seek to counsel or comfort Tamar, but allowed her to live desolate and isolated the rest of her life. Thirdly, David did not reprimand, punish, or hand over Amnon to the authorities. Churches must have the sensitivity to comfort and counsel the victims of sexual assault and have the courage and conviction to see that the abusers are punished accordingly.

JOSEPH

While the terminology may be different, the reality is Joseph was falsely accused of sexual assault in Genesis 39:11-15 (New International Version):

> *¹¹One day he went into the house to attend to his duties, and none of the household servants was inside. ¹² She caught him by his cloak and said, "Come to bed with me!" But he left his cloak in her hand and ran out of the house.*

> *¹³ When she saw that he had left his cloak in her hand and had run out of the house, ¹⁴ she called her household servants. "Look," she said to them, "this Hebrew has been brought to us to make sport of us! He came in here to sleep with me, but I screamed. ¹⁵ When he heard me scream for help, he left his cloak beside me and ran out of the house.*

As we all know, Joseph was placed in prison for a false accusation. While it is important to handle allegations seriously and swiftly, it is important for churches to not make a rush judgement without proper investigation. The scripture says in verse 19 and 20, "When his master heard the story his wife told him, saying, 'This is how your slave treated me', he burned with anger. Joseph's master took him and put him in prison, the place where the king's prisoners were confined."

There wasn't a trial, witnesses, or a jury. Potiphar heard one side of the story and immediately had Joseph placed in jail. The truth is, some accusations will be false.

In Joseph's case, sexual assault did take place, but the victim was not the woman, but the man. We must be mindful about rash judgments, assumptions and stereotypes about sexual assault victims and violators. While we mostly hear about sexual abuse involving adult men and young boys and girls, or sexual assault by adult men acting upon women, sexual assault and abuse can come in any combination—women molesting girls and boys, women harassing men, younger boys and girls harassing adult men and women, adult men harassing adult men, and adult women harassing adult women. We must recognize that all forms of unwanted sexual harassment, abuse, and assault are totally unacceptable in the church.

BATHSHEBA

2 Samuel 11 records a different episode of sexual assault in the Bible. This time it involves King David. David, abusing his authority as king, kidnapped, raped, and fathered a child by another man's wife. To cover it up, he had her husband killed in battled so he could ultimately marry the woman. What is most notable about this story is found in 2 Samuel 12 when Nathan confronts David about his sins. One of the most quoted phrases in the Bible, Nathan, risking his life and livelihood tells David, "Thou art the man."

The LORD sent Nathan to David. When he came to him, he said,

"There were two men in a certain town, one rich and the other poor.² The rich man had a very large number of sheep and cattle, ³ but the poor man had nothing except one little ewe lamb he had bought. He raised it, and it grew up with him and his children. It shared his food, drank from his cup and even slept in his arms. It was like a daughter to him.

⁴ "Now a traveler came to the rich man, but the rich man refrained from taking one of his own sheep or cattle to prepare a meal for the traveler who had come to him. Instead, he took the ewe lamb that belonged to the poor man and prepared it for the one who had come to him."

⁵ David burned with anger against the man and said to Nathan, "As surely as the LORD lives, the man who did this must die! ⁶ He must pay for that lamb four times over, because he did such a thing and had no pity."

⁷ Then Nathan said to David, "You are the man! This is what the LORD, the God of Israel, says: 'I anointed you king over Israel, and I delivered you from the hand of Saul. ⁸ I gave your master's house to you, and your master's wives into your arms. I gave you all Israel and Judah. And if all this had been too little, I would have given you even more. ⁹ Why did you despise the word of the LORD by doing what is evil in his eyes? You struck down Uriah the Hittite with the sword and took his wife to be your own. You killed him with the sword of the Ammonites. ¹⁰ Now, therefore, the sword will never depart from your house, because you despised me and took the wife of Uriah the Hittite to be your own.'

[11] *"This is what the L*ORD* says: 'Out of your own household I am going to bring calamity on you. Before your very eyes I will take your wives and give them to one who is close to you, and he will sleep with your wives in broad daylight.* [12] *You did it in secret, but I will do this thing in broad daylight before all Israel.'"*

[13] *Then David said to Nathan, "I have sinned against the L*ORD*."*

*Nathan replied, "The L*ORD* has taken away your sin. You are not going to die.* [14] *But because by doing this you have shown utter contempt for*[a]*the L*ORD*, the son born to you will die"* (New International Version).

Yes, grace, mercy, and redemption is possible for those who commit sexual abuse and assault, but thank God for bold, courageous, spirit-led prophets that can speak to authority figures and tell them what thus sayeth the Lord. David was told of his sins and repented for them, but also accepted the full consequences of his actions declared to him by the Prophet Nathan. Preachers: don't be afraid to take a bold stand to preach out against, not just homosexuality, fornication, and adultery, but against molestation, sexual harassment, sexual assault and child abuse. Regardless of the popularity, prominence, tenure, gifting or influence of the pastor, preacher, or member who commits sexual abuse or assault, the church must not be afraid to confront and properly deal with David!

DINAH

Most Bible students know the 12 sons or tribes of Israel, but often forget about the one daughter of Jacob, named Dinah. Genesis 34 (New International Version) records her rape by the Shechemite man.

> *Now Dinah, the daughter Leah had borne to Jacob, went out to visit the women of the land. ² When Shechem son of Hamor the Hivite, the ruler of that area, saw her, he took her and raped her. ³ His heart was drawn to Dinah daughter of Jacob; he loved the young woman and spoke tenderly to her. ⁴ And Shechem said to his father Hamor, "Get me this girl as my wife."*

ll of the men, who went out of the city gate, agreed with Hamor and his son Shechem, and every male in the city was circumcised.

> *²⁵ Three days later, while all of them were still in pain, two of Jacob's sons, Simeon and Levi, Dinah's brothers, took their swords and attacked the unsuspecting city, killing every male. ²⁶ They put Hamor and his son Shechem to the sword and took Dinah from Shechem's house and left.²⁷ The sons of Jacob came upon the dead bodies and looted the city where[c] their sister had been defiled. ²⁸ They seized their flocks and herds and donkeys and everything else of theirs in the city and out in the fields. ²⁹ They carried off all their wealth and all their women and children, taking as plunder everything in the houses.*

A few points from this passage of scripture: (1) sexual assault and abuse not only involve individuals, but also families on both sides of the situation. While families do not necessarily have the right to negotiate a settlement agreement for a sexual assault or child abuse case, do not overlook the fact both victims and abusers have families and that the church will often have to work with multiple family members, multiple personalities, multiple emotions, and multiple opinions when dealing with a sexual assault matter. Multiple meetings and counseling may be required, not just for the victim and the violator, but the victim's families and the violator's family, especially when both families are members of the same church. Even when the relationship is consensual between two teenagers in the church, there can be a complete war between the two families because of the situation. In many cases, the family of the accused will experience shame, ridicule, guilt, and isolations for what their family member did to someone else. When possible, the church should try to maintain peace and prevent the slaughter of "Shecem's family" within our congregations.

THE LEVITE AND HIS CONCUBINE

Judges 19 (New International Version) records a time of lawlessness in the land of Israel. The passage starts by saying that it was a time in which Israel had no king. To make a long story short, the husband is traveling with his wife to go to the house of the Lord. Agreeing to spend the night at someone's house on his journey, the scripture states,

22 While they were enjoying themselves, some of the wicked men of the city surrounded the house. Pounding on the door, they shouted to the old man who owned the house, "Bring out the man who came to your house so we can have sex with him."

23 The owner of the house went outside and said to them, "No, my friends, don't be so vile. Since this man is my guest, don't do this outrageous thing. 24 Look, here is my virgin daughter, and his concubine. I will bring them out to you now, and you can use them and do to them whatever you wish. But as for this man, don't do such an outrageous thing."

25 But the men would not listen to him. So the man took his concubine and sent her outside to them, and they raped her and abused her throughout the night, and at dawn they let her go. 26 At daybreak the woman went back to the house where her master was staying, fell down at the door and lay there until daylight.

27 When her master got up in the morning and opened the door of the house and stepped out to continue on his way, there lay his concubine, fallen in the doorway of the house, with her hands on the threshold.28 He said to her, "Get up; let's go." But there was no answer. Then the man put her on his donkey and set out for home.

29 When he reached home, he took a knife and cut up his concubine, limb by limb, into twelve parts and sent them into all the areas of Israel.30 Everyone who saw it was saying to one another, "Such a thing has never been seen or done, not since the day the Israelites came up out of Egypt. Just imagine! We must do something! So speak up!"

In applying this passage to the current conversation, the question that can be raised, "When is it appropriate for the entire congregation to know about a private matter of sexual assault and abuse?" While privacy is important, there will be times in which the entire congregation must be made aware and informed of a horrific situation. This is not for the congregation to have new information for rumor, gossip, or slander, but to request privacy, confidentially, and prayers for the parties involved in the situation. It also may provide the congregation with a "teachable moment" to educate the church on issues of sex abuse and assault, scriptures related to the situation and church policy, as it relates to such matters. Not that a church should humiliate anyone or make all information public, but it may be necessary for a congregation to see how sexual harassment and assault matters are handled in an open, honest, fair, impartial, timely and transparent manner. Members may have to be educated on how to deal with the community, media and more specifically social media, as the public may learn about certain events that may have transpired in a church. In many cases, if the matter is already out in the public, then it may be easier, but also necessary, to deal with it publicly. If a sex offender joins a church, it will be important that, at least key leaders, are informed and charged with monitoring the individual. In other words, there will be times when "Israel" will need to know and be called upon to take appropriate action.

CORINTHIANS

The Apostle Paul in I Corinthians 5:1-5 (New International Version) writes,

> It is actually reported that there is sexual immorality among you, and of a kind that even pagans do not tolerate: A man is sleeping with his father's wife.
>
> ² And you are proud! Shouldn't you rather have gone into mourning and have put out of your fellowship the man who has been doing this?
>
> ³ For my part, even though I am not physically present, I am with you in spirit. As one who is present with you in this way, I have already passed judgment in the name of our Lord Jesus on the one who has been doing this.
>
> ⁴ So when you are assembled and I am with you in spirit, and the power of our Lord Jesus is present,
>
> ⁵ hand this man overto Satan for the destruction of the flesh,[a][b] so that his spirit may be saved on the day of the Lord.

What we do know about the situation in the Corinthian church is that the matter Paul was addressing involved sexual immorality, in particular incest - a man who had married his father's wife. What is perhaps up to debate is the meaning and implications of Paul's instructions to "hand this man over to Satan for the destruction of the flesh." If interpreted as many do, this scripture permits the church to actually remove a member for sexual immorality. Is it reasonable to conclude that an unrepentant, untransformed, reprobate sex offender should not only be removed from a position of authority in the church but also from the church itself? While this should be the choice of last resort, it is understandable, if not required, to ask a sex offender to leave a congregation if new allegations of abuse and assault in the church are proven to be true.

Admittedly, the church finds itself in a difficult position. How can the church be open to all types of people, yet be protective of everyone at the same time? How can a church have tight security and screening, like an airport, but be as open and accessible to the public as the local grocery store? Although scripture tells us that Christ is coming back for a church without a spot or wrinkle, the truth remains that the church remains a place where people of mixed levels of faith, maturity, sinful practices, and proclivities come together on a regular basis. Unlike a school or a corporation that can immediately run a background check or move to suspend or terminate an employee, churches do not screen its members nor can easily terminate a member.

However, churches must be wise and institute policies to protect its members, and at a minimum, ensure that those in volunteer or leadership positions have been properly vetted, screened and trained. Churches must also take affirmative steps to immediately investigate an accusation. If a person is found guilty, a church must take appropriate action—reprimand, suspend, remove from position, terminate membership, and where warranted, refer to legal authorities for further action. Churches should adopt a zero-tolerance policy for sexual assault and abuse as it relates to volunteers and those in leadership positions.

While the sex offender needs salvation too, churches must make the distinction between salvation and service. A church cannot turn away a sex offender who has genuinely repented and is seeking salvation. However, churches must be wise to implement appropriate safe guards and prohibit former sex offenders from holding certain positions in the church.

As Love and Norris writes, "Sexual predators will gravitate to activities and organizations where fewer protective measures are in place. The church should lead the way in promoting a protective culture that is easily seen, obvious to parent and offender alike... When a pro-active church communicates effectively, sexual offenders will opt out of church programming, because 'it's just too hard here'. Perhaps someday offender access will be 'too hard' in every church."

Expounding upon this point, Love and Norris, provide five specific components to create an effective church safety system including training, screening, background checks, tailored policies, and effective monitoring. In addition to this list, church leaders must be aware of laws related to reporting sexual abuse to law enforcement officials.[4] Church

---

[4] Reporting requirement for clergy vary from state to state as it relates to child abuse. Some states provide an absolute privilege of confidential communication between a minister and the victim or abuser. On the other hand, some states mandate that clergy report known or suspected instances of child abuse to authorities in a manner similar to school teachers and healthcare professionals. In addition to reviewing you state code, I recommend for further reading, https://www.childwelfare.gov/pubPDFs/clergymandated.pdf

leaders must be willing to seek the assistance of outside help, such as licensed and trained professional, to provide counseling to those impacted by the sexual abuse. Church leaders must be led by the spirit in discerning of potential problem and handling them with wisdom and care.

Further, church leaders must be better trained to deal with, and be sensitive to the issues of those that have been abused and assaulted. With research indicating that one out of three girls and one out of seven boys will be sexually abused before the age of 18, these victims will become members of our congregations. They may come to the church perfectly fine, while others may come with marital problems, drug addictions, mental illness, and alternative lifestyles because of what happened to them as children. Churches must have ministries and counselors prepared to minister to the survivors of sexual assault and abuse. God wants to transform victims into being not just mere survivors, but actual overcomers of their past negative experiences!

If church leaders are proactive, observant, wise, and spirit-led, the church can properly deal with the polar bear problem in the church.

Discussion Questions

(1) When is it appropriate for the entire congregation to know about a private matter of sexual assault and abuse involving members of the church?

(2) What policies do you have for screening volunteers?

(3) What technology and practices do you use to ensure the safety of members from sexual abuse and assault?

(4) What are the requirements in your state for clergy in reporting child abuse?

(5) How can a church protect and minister to families on both sides of a sexual abuse case?

(6) How can the church welcome and minister to sex offenders and protect itself against a future instance of sex abuse?

(7) How do you determine the right level of punishment in a sexual harassment or assault case? When is it appropriate to reprimand, suspend, terminate or refer to authorities an allegation of sexual harassment or assault?

(8) What ministries are in place to serve past and current victims of sexual assault and abuse that attend your church?

(9) How can a church empathize with a victim of sexual abuse, but not enable them to continue living in deviant or destructive lifestyles?

(10) Is it ever proper to remove someone from your church? If so, under what conditions and how should it be done properly?

(11) Describe your processes for handling allegations of sexual assault or harassment in your church. To whom should it be reported to first? Where does it go from there? Who hears or adjudicates the matter and makes a decision on what should be done to the individual if it is true? Do members in your church know the process? Is it documented anywhere?

References

Clergy as Mandatory Reporters of Child abuse and neglect
https://www.childwelfare.gov/pubPDFs/clergymandated.pdf

The Religious Community Is Speaking Out Against Sexual Violence With #ChurchToo
http://time.com/5034546/me-too-church-too-sexual-abuse/

Sexual Harassment In Church
http://www.calltherightattorney.com/2013/06/03/sexual-harassment-in-church/

SEXUAL HARASSMENT AND THE CHURCH: SEXUAL HARASSMENT IN THE CHURCH
https://youthspecialties.com/blog/sexual-harassment-and-the-church-sexual-harassment-in-the-church/

How to Spot Sexual Abuse in Your Church
https://www.christianitytoday.com/pastors/2015/january-online-only/how-to-spot-sexual-abuse-in-your-church.html

Startling Statistics: Child sexual abuse and what the church can begin doing about it
https://religionnews.com/2014/01/09/startling-statistics/

Honesty and Ethics Rating of Clergy Slides to New Low
http://news.gallup.com/poll/166298/honesty-ethics-rating-clergy-slides-new-low.aspx

Trust in clergy in US declines to historic low, Gallup poll finds
https://www.christiantimes.com/article/trust-in-clergy-in-us-declines-to-historic-low-gallup-poll-finds/73490.htm

Why Megachurch Pastors Keep Falling Into Sexual Immorality
https://jenniferleclaire.org/articles/why-megachurch-pastors-keep-falling-into-sexual-immorality/

Exclusive Video: Polar Bear Cannibalizes Cub
https://news.nationalgeographic.com/2016/02/160223-polar-bears-arctic-cannibals-animals-science/

Polar Bear Eats Cub: Cannibalism May Be On The Rise
https://www.huffingtonpost.com/2011/12/08/polar-bear-eats-cub-cannibalism_n_1136428.html

Is Global Warming Driving Polar Bears to Cannibalism?
https://www.yahoo.com/news/global-warming-driving-polar-bears-cannibalism-185605556.html

Polar bear cannibalism and sea ice, the spring of 1976
https://polarbearscience.com/2013/10/30/polar-bear-cannibalism-and-sea-ice-the-spring-of-1976/

Polar Bear Turns Cannibal, Eats Its Own Cub In Front Of Mother
https://www.inquisitr.com/2823782/polar-bear-turns-cannibal-eats-its-own-cub-in-front-of-mother-video/

The Do's and Don'ts of Dealing with Sex Offenders at Church
https://www.guideone.com/dos-donts-dealing-sex-offenders-church/

Dealing with Sex Offenders Who Attend Church
http://www.churchlawandtax.com/web/2010/january/q14.html

Sexual abuse in the church: not just a "Catholic problem"
https://thinkchristian.reframemedia.com/sexual-abuse-in-the-church-not-just-a-catholic-problem

Sexual Harassment In The Church: Apology 'Has Never Been Enough'
https://www.npr.org/2018/01/14/578032206/sexual-harassment-in-the-church-apology-has-never-been-enough

DEALING WITH SEXUAL ABUSE IN THE CHURCH: ADVICE FOR PASTORS
https://sharperiron.org/article/dealing-with-sexual-abuse-church-advice-for-pastors

Survey: Christian Women Report Sexual Misconduct at Church
https://www.christianpost.com/news/survey-christian-women-report-sexual-misconduct-at-church-33927/

CHAPTER 7

THE KING COBRA

While often living in seclusion, the King Cobra is one of the most revered and feared cannibalistic animals. The King Cobra Snake is the largest venomous snake in the world and considered the most dangerous, especially to humans. In various parts of the world, snakes have been worshipped for centuries. The King Cobra is known for its length, growing up to 18 feet long. When attacked, a King Cobra will fan open its hood, standing at nearly six feet tall, and emanate an intimidating hiss to scare off the threat. Using smell, sight, and vibrations, the cobra is able to detect prey hundreds of feet away. Like other snakes, cobras eat their victim by enlarging their mouths and swallowing their victims head-first, without chewing. Strong acids in the snake's stomach will digest the food over several weeks depending on the size of the meal. While cobras primarily eat other types of snakes and small vertebrates, such as lizards, cobras are also known for being cannibalistic animals.

One of the key features of the king cobra is its toxic venom. Depending on the type of cobra it is, these animals have the ability to shoot toxic venom, with near perfect accuracy, into the eyes of its victim up to eight feet away. The venom in a king cobra is not the most toxic of venomous snakes, however, it has the ability to inject the largest amount.

"King Cobra venom attacks the victim's nervous system and quickly induces severe pain, blurred vision, vertigo, drowsiness and paralysis. In the minutes following, cardiovascular collapse occurs and the victim falls into a coma. Death soon follows due to respiratory failure."

The mortality rate from venom in humans can be as high as 75 percent. One injection of venom by a king cobra into a human being is enough to kill 20 adults.

King cobras are intimidating because of its size and stature, as well as its threat to other snakes, cobras, lizards, elephants, and humans. Its most lethal weapon is its toxic venom. The venom that is present in many churches today is the toxic venom of racism and classism.

The Reverend Martin Luther King, Jr. once said, "It is appalling that the most segregated hour of Christian America is eleven o'clock on Sunday morning." The question is this: how much has changed since the assassination of Dr. King in 1968? Are people of diverse ethnic, racial, economic, and educational levels welcomed in your church? While laws and court decisions forced schools, corporations, and neighborhoods to diversify, the church has been left relatively "untouched", and "unchanged", over the last century.

The Multiracial Congregations Project led by Michael Emerson, a Rice University sociologist, defines a multiracial congregation as one where no one racial group is more than 80% of the congregation. Using that standard, Emerson has found that only 8% of all Christian congregations in the U.S. are racially mixed to a significant degree: 2-3% of mainline Protestant congregations, 8% of other Protestant congregations, and 20% of Catholic parishes.

In a book, written by Steven R. Haynes, entitled, *The Last Segregated Hour*, he reports that although congregations are more diverse today (86 percent) than they were years ago, the change has been very small (97 percent). Haynes goes on to report that most churches are content with the status quo and have no desire to change in terms of racial diversity.

A Recent LifeWay research study reported "two-thirds of American churchgoers (67 percent) say their church has done enough to become racially diverse. And less than half think their church should become more diverse."

David R. Williams, "The Right Thing to Do," *Adventist Review*, on February 20, 1997, reported that "there is more racial prejudice in the Christian church than outside it, that church members are more prejudiced than nonmembers, that churchgoers are more biased than those who do not attend, and that regular attenders are more prejudiced than those who attend less often. It has been also been shown that persons who hold conservative theological beliefs are more likely to be prejudiced than those who do not."

Much finger pointing goes around when it comes to this topic. Blacks often blame whites for racism, discrimination, and exclusions. However, studies have indicated that blacks often prefer to worship in congregations where they are the majority. A recent book by Beverly Tatum, *Why Are All the Black Kids Sitting Together in the Cafeteria? And Other Conversations About Race,* seems relevant to this issue. Tatum claims that people need significant places and times to develop their own sense of identity, including racial identity. For whites, these opportunities are pervasive, since racial sameness is the norm of experience for whites. But for Blacks, she claims, these opportunities need to be established and protected, since racial otherness is the norm of experience for Blacks in America. Perhaps Black churches play a valuable role for Black life, one for which there is no comparable need in white life. Yet surprisingly, 51 percent of African Americans said that their church needs to become more ethnically diverse, compared to only 37 percent of whites in the survey (Lifeway Survey).

Hence, we have a conundrum. If everyone agrees that our churches are too segregated, but everyone likes their segregated churches, or feels that they have done enough to diversify their churches, will things ever change? And more importantly, are we required to change?

While over 2300 scriptures speak to the poor, widow, alien, etc., does the scripture speak to ethnic, racial, and class diversity in the church? What does the Bible say about racial and economic diversity in our churches?

Jesus, in the Great Commission said,

"Go ye therefore, and teach all nations, baptizing them in the name of the Father, and of the Son, and of

the Holy Ghost: Teaching them to observe all things whatsoever I have commanded you: and, lo, I am with you always, even unto the end of the world. Amen"

—(Matthew 28:19-20, King James Version).

For many churches, the issue of outreach and evangelism to the poor, or people of another race or nationality, is not an issue. Money and ministries have been devoted to sharing faith with the poor and spreading the gospel in both the United States and foreign countries. However, having those same people to join a congregation or become a permanent member of the church family is unthinkable. The "separate-but-equal, we can ride the same bus, but sit in separate sections", still exists. Some Christians dream of sharing the gospel in foreign lands but could never imagine sitting next to those same people on a pew in their home church. How have we accepted this mentality that it is alright to share our faith with others, yet reject the idea of worshipping together in the same church?

To illustrate the point of classism in the church, in recent years, many churches have built brand new state of the art facilities in the suburbs away from poor people and minority groups. While legitimate factors such as cost, convenience to existing members, safety, and availability of land can impact a decision, it should never be the goal of a church to move, simply to get away from a certain demographic of people. Many churches leave without providing local residents with transportation to the suburbs or a smaller satellite outreach ministry in the neighborhood. As businesses and sports arenas are moving back into the inner cities to revitalize the city, the church should be on the forefront of such urban renewal and revitalization—not running from the problem.

When we read the book of Acts, we find that God always intended for his church to be a place of diversity and inclusion. At the ascension, Jesus said, "But ye shall receive power, after that the Holy Ghost is come upon you: and ye shall be witnesses unto me both in Jerusalem, and in all Judaea, and in Samaria, and unto the uttermost part of the earth" (Acts 1:8, King James Version). On the day of Pentecost, we read, "Parthians, and Medes, and Elamites, and the dwellers in Mesopotamia, and in Judaea, and Cappadocia, in Pontus, and Asia, Phrygia, and Pamphylia, in Egypt, and in the parts of Libya about Cyrene, and strangers of Rome, Jews and proselytes Cretes and Arabians, we do hear them speak in our tongues the wonderful works of God" (Acts 2:9-11, King James Version). Yet coincidentally, the first dispute to arise in the early church involved not only church administration but implicitly, it also involved issues of racism and class discrimination. It was the poor Grecian widows that were been neglected in the daily ministration while the poor Hebrew widows were being served. (See Acts 6:1-4). However, from Pentecost, we read of Samaritans, Ethiopians, and Gentiles all receiving the same gospel and being joined to the same church.

Yet, in reviewing the history of Christianity in America, we find that the church has struggled to maintain racial and economic unity. In 1816, Richard Allen split from the predominately white, United Methodist Church, to form the predominately black, African Methodist Episcopal Church. In 1845, white southerners split to form the Southern Baptist Church over the issue of slavery. In 1880, Rev. Elias Camp Morris formed the National Baptist Convention, the largest predominately black Baptist fellowship. While the modern American Pentecostalism movement started with great optimism of being a racially unified church, eventually social and cultural pressures would divide the church. The Assembly of God withdrew from the Church of God in Christ in 1914. White ministers and congregations left the Pentecostal Assemblies of the World, during the 1920's, to form a predominantly white oneness-Pentecostal fellowship organization, now known as the United Pentecost Church International. Similarly, in the 1920's, Hispanics formed the Apostolic Assembly of the Faith in Christ Jesus, which today stands as the oldest Spanish-speaking, oneness-Pentecostal fellowship organization. Although the Catholic church has not necessarily split, it is no secret that racial divisions between African, Latino, Asian, and European-American churches exist. Perhaps it can be understood that the political and cultural issues of the time caused these denominational splits, but the question becomes, "Why after decades, have these splits remained intact?" Rick Warren, in a recent interview, states that racism is the one thing preventing revival in America.

Paul writes in Galatians, "For ye are all the children of God by faith in Christ Jesus. For as many of you as have been baptized into Christ have put on Christ. There is neither Jew nor Greek, there is neither bond nor free, there is neither male nor female: for ye are all one in Christ Jesus" (Galatians 5:27-29, King James Version). In Revelations, John writes, "After this I looked, and there before me was a great multitude that no one could count, from every nation, tribe, people and language, standing before the throne and before the Lamb. They were wearing white robes and were holding palm branches in their hands. And they cried out in a loud voice: 'Salvation belongs to our God, who sits on the throne, and to the Lamb'" (Revelation 7:9-11, New International Version). In reading these scriptures, we realize that there is only one church, not a black, white, Hispanic, Asian, affluent, or poor-people's church, but one church, purchased by the shed blood of Jesus Christ. If the church is to reflect the worship and diversity that we will experience in Heaven, then the church can no longer tolerate or accept a racially divided body on Earth.

Billy Graham remarked in an article that even though racial and ethnic hostility is the number one social problem facing the world and the church, "evangelical Christians have turned a blind eye to racism or have been willing to stand aside while others take the lead in racial reconciliation, saying it was not our responsibility." [6]. He goes on to say, "Racial or ethnic prejudice is a sin in the eyes of God, and no Christian should allow his or her heart to be filled with prejudice."

A survey found in Christianity Today suggest that while almost all (90 percent) of senior pastors say racial reconciliation is mandated by the gospel, only four in 10 (43 percent) say they speak on the issue once a year or less. Twenty-nine percent of pastors rarely or never do.

Pastors and church leaders must address the issue head-on as James wrote to the church,

"My brothers and sisters, believers in our glorious Lord Jesus Christ must not show favoritism. Suppose a man comes into your meeting wearing a gold ring and fine clothes, and a poor man in filthy old clothes also comes in. If you show special attention to the man wearing fine clothes and say, "Here's a good seat for you," but say to the poor man, "You stand there" or "Sit on the floor by my feet," have you not discriminated among yourselves and become judges with evil thoughts? Listen, my dear brothers and sisters: Has not God chosen those who are poor in the eyes of the world to be rich in faith and to inherit the kingdom he promised those who love him? But you have dishonored the poor. Is it not the rich who are exploiting you? Are they not the ones who are dragging you into court? Are they not the ones who are blaspheming the noble name of him to whom you belong? If you really keep the royal law found in Scripture, "Love your neighbor as yourself,"[a] you are doing right. But if you show favoritism, you sin and are convicted by the law as lawbreakers. For whoever keeps the whole law and yet stumbles at just one point is guilty of breaking all of it"

–(James 2:1-10, New International Version).

Churches and church leaders must work together and realize that a racially and economically divided church is not pleasing to God and can no longer be accepted as "normal". The church can no longer allow the schools, courts, athletic fields, and corporations to take the lead on this matter. Things will not change until it is addressed head-on, on a consistent basis, from the pulpit. If the church can preach on abortion, homosexuality, divorce, drugs, poverty, and even racism, but not take systematic steps to bring racial and economic diversity into our congregations, it will never change. Until we see segregated churches as a sin and abomination before God as other evils, we will continue to give Satan victory over the church.

Discussion Questions

(1) What is the racial composition of your church?

(2) How often do people of a different race visit your church? How many have actually joined? How many actually stayed more than one year? Have members of a diverse race ever joined your church?

(3) How often does your church fellowship with churches of a different race or invite speakers or psalmists from other races or ethnicities to your church?

(4) What strategic and intentional activities and ministries have been established in your church to reach a more diverse crowd?

(5) How often are issues of racism, class, racial reconciliation, and diversity discussed, taught, or preached about in your church?

(6) How diverse is your church in terms of class and economic status? Do poor and less educated people feel welcomed into your church? Do wealthy and more educated people feel welcomed into your church?

(7) What aspects of worship would have to be changed to attract or appeal to a more diverse audience?

(8) Does your church have a reputation for only being for blacks, whites, Asians, or Hispanics? Does your church have a reputation for only being for the elite, wealthy, or well educated? How did your church gain this reputation? Is it true? Can it or should it be changed? How can it be changed?

(9) Why do you think that Sunday at 11 a.m. is still the most segregated time in America?

(10) Do you agree with Billy Graham that evangelical Christians have turned a blind eye to racism or have been willing to stand aside while others take the lead in racial reconciliation, saying it is not our responsibility?

(11) Do you agree with Pastor Rick Warren that "racism is the one thing preventing revival in America"?

References

RACISM AND THE CHURCH
http://www.drpipim.org/church-racism-contemporaryissues-51/102-racism-and-the-church.html

Sunday Morning Segregation: Most Worshipers Feel Their Church Has Enough Diversity
http://www.christianitytoday.com/news/2015/january/sunday-morning-segregation-most-worshipers-church-diversity.html

Membership Is Not Cheap: Classism in the Church
http://stevesbasics.blogspot.com/2014/05/membership-is-not-cheap-classism-in.html

The Most Segregated Hour in America?
http://www.phil.vt.edu/JKlagge/ConductorChurch.htm

COBRA
http://www.kidzone.ws/lw/snakes/facts-cobra.htm
King Cobras Are Cannibals
http://www.myamazingearth.com/2017/01/king-cobras-are-cannibals.html

King cobras fall into pit, female swallows mate
https://timesofindia.indiatimes.com/home/environment/flora-fauna/King-cobras-fall-into-pit-female-swallows-mate/articleshow/46256804.cms

The Secrets of the King Cobra: The Cannibal Snake
http://readerslab.blogspot.com/2012/03/secrets-of-king-cobra-cannibal-snake.html

Cobras Spit Venom at Eyes With Nearly Perfect Aim
https://news.nationalgeographic.com/news/2005/02/0210_050210_cobra_2.html

King Cobra Snakes
https://animalcorner.co.uk/animals/king-cobra-snakes/

RACISM AND THE CHURCH
http://www.drpipim.org/church-racism-contemporaryissues-51/102-racism-and-the-church.html

10 TOP REASONS RACISM CONTINUES IN THE CHURCH TODAY
https://www.emotionallyhealthy.org/10-top-reasons-racism-continues-in-the-church-today/

CHAPTER 8

THE ORANGUTAN

2 *And you hath he quickened, who were dead in trespasses and sins;* [2] *Wherein in time past ye walked according to the course of this world, according to the prince of the power of the air, the spirit that now worketh in the children of disobedience:* [3] *Among whom also we all had our conversation in times past in the lusts of our flesh, fulfilling the desires of the flesh and of the mind; and were by nature the children of wrath, even as others.* [4] *But God, who is rich in mercy, for his great love wherewith he loved us,* [5] *Even when we were dead in sins, hath quickened us together with Christ, (by grace ye are saved;)* [6] *And hath raised us up together, and made us sit together in heavenly places in Christ Jesus:* [7] *That in the ages to come he might shew the exceeding riches of his grace in his kindness toward us through Christ Jesus.* [8] *For by grace are ye saved through faith; and that not of yourselves: it is the gift of God:* [9] *Not of works, lest any man should boast.* [10] *For we are his workmanship, created in Christ Jesus unto good works, which God hath before ordained that we should walk in them.* [11] *Wherefore* *remember, that ye being in time past Gentiles in the flesh, who are called Uncircumcision by that which is called the Circumcision in the flesh made by hands;*[12] *That at that time ye were without Christ, being aliens from the commonwealth of Israel, and strangers from the covenants of promise, having no hope, and without God in the world:* [13] *But now in Christ Jesus ye who sometimes were far off are made nigh by the blood of Christ.* [14] *For he is our peace, who hath made both one, and hath broken down the middle wall of partition between us;* [15] *Having abolished in his flesh the enmity, even the law of commandments contained in ordinances; for to make in himself of twain one new man, so making peace;*[16] *And that he might reconcile both unto God in one body by the cross, having slain the enmity thereby:* [17] *And came and preached peace to you which were afar off, and to them that were nigh.* [18] *For through him we both have access by one Spirit unto the Father.* [19] *Now therefore ye are no more strangers and foreigners, but fellow citizens with the saints, and of the household of God;* [20] *And are built upon the foundation of the apostles and prophets, Jesus Christ himself being the chief corner stone;* [21] *In whom all the building fitly framed together groweth unto an holy temple in the Lord:*[22] *In whom ye also are builded together for an habitation of God through the Spirit"*

—(Ephesians 2, King James Version).

This scripture leads us into the discussion of one of our final cannibalistic animals: the orangutan. Unlike many of the other animals that kill and then consume one of its own species, two orangutans, in a recent study, were observed to consume over a period of time, their deceased infants.

The first, after carrying around her deceased infant on her back for seven days, began the process of eating her infant. It was noted that before and after consumption began, this orangutan would periodically remove and inspect the corpse that she carried on her back, occasionally emitting a whimper. The corpse was consumed in its entirety over a period of three days. Similarly, in the second case, the orangutan was seen eating her deceased infant after carrying it around for a period of time. It had been observed that the infant had been unwell and unresponsive for a few days before death. In both cases, no evidence suggests that the mother harmed or killed their infant prior to consuming it.

After learning about the orangutan, the Lord asked me a question, "What are you doing with the spiritually sick and dead?" For the orangutan, it was only two options: bury or consume. However, for the church, we have a third option: to restore back to life. Paul writes in Galatians 6:1 (King James Version), "Brethren, if a man be overtaken in a fault, ye which are spiritual, restore such an one in the spirit of meekness; considering thyself, lest thou also be tempted". My question to you is this: is your church open to sinners and backsliders?

Author Zac Poonen writes that in Luke 15, Jesus speaks about four types of backsliders: lost sheep, the lost coin, the lost younger son and the lost elder son. Poonen elaborates by stating that the parable of the lost sheep represents the born-again believer that strays away or is pulled away from the church. It is up to the shepherd to find and bring back this lost sheep into the fold. In the parable of the lost coin, the woman represents the church's carelessness. We have not taken care of the coin (redeemed souls). The lost coin will only be found with proper light and extensive cleaning. The parable of the prodigal son represents two types of backsliders: the prodigal son and the elder brother. The prodigal son represents those who outright rebel against God and his church, while the elder brother represents one who remains in the house (church), but are in a backslidden state. What possibly makes the elder brother worse than the others is because he does not recognize that his pride, self-righteousness, and jealousy has created un-repented sin in his life. For the rebellious son, the church or shepherd does not go after him. However, when he returns in true brokenness and repentance, the church must be wide open to welcome him and restore him. With the elder son, it was the preaching and teaching of the father that led him back to the house.

Regardless of how a person fell, backslid, strayed away, or rebelled against God, the question remains the same: are we willing to restore such a one in the spirit of meekness, or do we take on the attitude of the Pharisees that, "this one is not good enough to be associated with us." Are unwed mothers, felons, divorcees, drug-addicts, prostitutes, and unmarried-cohabitating couples received in our churches? Can one with tattoos, body piercings, unique hairstyles, and abhorrent lifestyles be invited and received into our congregations with love, grace, and patience? Would the atheist, agnostic, Muslim, or member of the LGBT community feel genuine love and have an authentic encounter with God at your church? If one visits or stops attending our church, are there people in the congregation who are assigned to reach out, follow-up, or pray for them? Are we committed to finding the lost sheep and searching for the lost coin? Is evangelism and outreach just a committee, event, or an activity? Or is it an attitude and mission of the church? Alternatively, do we want people who are squeaky-clean and come from picture-perfect families, flawless backgrounds, and mistake-less lives? Is the church truly a hospital for sinners or a museum of saints?

The church must be aware of any rules (written or unwritten), doctrines, traditions, practices, or subliminal messages that may be keeping a backslider from feeling welcomed in our church. Many churches have unwritten codes, similar to black codes and segregation laws of the past, that suggest that church is for "saints-only" and all others are not welcomed. Do we preach the truth in love or do we preach to attack, humiliate, and belittle people? While we do not condone the sin, we do not condemn the sinner. We must embrace the message of Jesus to the woman caught in the act of adultery, "Go in peace and sin no more!"

Further, a church does not have to completely change its culture to become a seeker-sensitive congregation, but it should be aware of any issues that the church can address that may prevent a church from being considered welcoming to sinners and backsliders. Unfortunately, many churches are like the orangutan that cries about her deceased infant, but consumes it at the same time. The church can no longer hypocritically cry in prayer for sinners while our actions kill and devour those God sends to us for restoration.

The goal of the church is not to see how many people it can condemn and send to hell, but how many people it can rescue from the flames of hell. John 3:16-17 tell us, "For God so loved the world, that he gave his only begotten Son, that whosoever believeth in him should not perish, but have everlasting life. For God sent not his Son into the world to condemn the world; but that the world through him might be saved." Understand that Jesus did not die for saints, but He died for sinners in order for them to become saints. Romans 5:8 reminds us, "But God commendeth his love toward us, in that, while we were yet sinners, Christ died for us." Jude goes on to write, And of some have compassion, making a difference: And others save with fear, pulling them out of the fire; hating even the garment spotted by the flesh" (King James Version).

The reality is that churches grow three ways: new births, transfers, and converts. Consequently, churches also lose members three ways: deaths, transfers, and backsliding. Many churches have become content with growing, simply by births and transfers. Many churches have embraced the microwave mentality, preferring prepped meals that only require "heating-up" before serving. Similarly, many churches only know how to take in microwavable members and do not have the time, energy, or effort to make saints from "scratch". However, the church must reconsider this ideology if it is to be successful in accomplishing the mission of the church: to convert the sinner and restore the backslider.

Matthew 9:10-13 records,

"Why does your teacher eat with tax collectors and sinners?" On hearing this, Jesus said, "It is not the healthy who need a doctor, but the sick. But go and learn what this means: 'I desire mercy, not sacrifice.' For I have not come to call the righteous, but sinners."

–(New International Version)

Discussion Questions

(1) What are rules doctrines, traditions, practices, or subliminal messages that may keep a backslider from feeling welcome in your church?

(2) Does your church have an organized follow-up system to reach out to people who are long-term absent or have left the ministry?

(3) How would you rate your church as an evangelistic ministry? What immediate steps could you take to make your church more evangelistic?

(4) Assess your current strategy for finding "the lost sheep" and searching for "the missing coin".

(5) Are those who left your ministry welcome back at any time? How have you communicated this message to them?

(6) How can your church become more seeker-sensitive without compromising its biblical identity?

(7) What percentage of new members in the past few years were by birth, transfer, or conversion?

(8) What percentage departed because of death, transfer due to relocation, transfer to join another local church, or departed, but not attending any church?

(9) How do you bridge the gap between the prodigal sons and elder brothers in the congregation?

References

The Church: A Place to Belong for Sinners
https://churchleaders.com/pastors/pastor-articles/138191-the-church-a-place-to-belong-for-sinners.html

The Church: Hospital For Sinners or Club For Saints?
https://everestalexander.wordpress.com/2015/02/04/the-church-hospital-for-sinners-or-club-for-saints/

Church—A Hospital For Sinners
http://soulwinning.info/articles/hospital_for_sinners.htm

A Church That Welcomes Sinners
https://corechristianity.com/resource-library/articles/a-church-that-welcomes-sinners

Pastor Leads A New Brand Of Church For 'Sinners And Saints'
https://www.npr.org/2013/12/20/255281434/pastor-leads-a-new-brand-of-church-for-sinners-and-saints

The church should be a hospital for sinners
https://www.ncronline.org/blogs/parish-diary/church-should-be-hospital-sinners

Is the Church for Sinners or Saints?
https://inallthings.org/is-the-church-for-sinner-or-saints/

Reaching Out To Backsliders
http://timmassengale.org/2015/10/reaching-out-to-backsliders/

Four Types Of Backsliders
http://www.cfcindia.com/article/four-types-of-backsliders

Two cases of mother-infant cannibalism in orangutans
http://www.orangutanhealth.org/res/file/Publications/Dellatore%20et%20al-%20Orangutan%20cannibalism.pdf

CHAPTER 9

THE PRAYING MANTIS

"The female praying mantis is often painted as an evil seductress, a cannibalistic lover who lures males closer only to eat them after mating." The praying mantis engages in a unique form of cannibalism, known as sexual cannibalism. With sexual cannibalism, the female species eats the male species before, during, or after mating. According to a study, in nature, male mantises are eaten by females in about 13-28 percent of sexual encounters. The male mantis decides to risk its life in exchange for a single chance to mate and reproduce.

After the male serves its copulatory purpose, the female often eats the head or legs of the smaller male mate. It has been observed that even when "beheaded," the male mantis is able to complete the process of reproduction. While the male mantis continues to inseminate the female, she begins the process of devouring him from head to toe. The male mantis never lets go, or stops having intercourse with the female mantis while his body is being consumed by her.

During mantis mating season, males can make up as much as 63 percent of the female diet. It is believed that in eating the male, a female ensures that the male continues to provide for the progeny, in the way of food, after its mate's death. The nutrients from the deceased male increase the chances of a healthy pregnancy and offspring.

By now you are either clueless or have already anticipated where this chapter in the book is heading. David Marrow, in his book entitled, *Why Men Hate Going to Church*, states, "more than 90 percent of American men believe in God, and five out of six call themselves Christians. But only two out of six attend church on a given Sunday. The average man accepts the reality of Jesus Christ, but fails to see any value in going to church."

According to a recent survey, men make up only 39 percent of the worshipers in a typical congregation. Of that group, many only come out of obligation to wives, mothers, or children. Many have blamed the style of worship, church attire, the length and time of the worship service, work schedules, offerings, hypocritical churches, insensitive pulpits, preaching styles, and the lack of males, in particular, fatherly role models (See 7 Reasons Why Men Don't Attend Church by Frederick Goodall). Yet, if this was the full explanation of why men do not go to church, one would think that women would also have the same issues with the church, especially when, for centuries, the church had been considered a sexist and oppressive institution for women.

While some would argue that men generally are not very religious, research into male participation in other world religions paints a contrasting picture. Marrow states, "male and female participation are roughly equal in

Judaism, Buddhism, and Hinduism. In the Islamic world, men are publicly and unashamedly religious—often more so than women. Of the world's great religions, only Christianity has a consistent, nagging shortage of male practitioners."

Thus, the question is this: is the failure of the church to attract and retain men an issue of men rejecting the requirements of Christianity—love, purity, forgiveness, repentance, and worship—for more manly pursuits such as career, sports, hobbies? Or is it a matter of the church over-catering to women and children in ministry focus, church décor, and teaching to the neglect or abandonment of male focused messages and ministries?

How can it be that the church, dominated by male leadership, has produced a seemingly overly-femininized church culture? Have we lost men, not because men are anti-religious, or because the church has numerous flaws, but because we have in fact "catered to the crowd" and failed to have a message and ministry that is attractive to men?

Not to stereotype men and women, but you may agree with some of the comparisons. A man would rather wash the car than wash dishes. A man would rather change the oil in the car than to change the baby's diaper. A man would rather fish and hunt for food than to roam the isles of a grocery store. A man would rather cook on the grill outside than bake a pie in the oven. A man would rather sit in a barbershop for 2 hours, waiting for a haircut, than sit in a church service for the same amount of time.

These examples illustrate a simple point: it's not that men will not "go and do", but will likely prefer to "go and do" them in a manner different than women. Men typically like challenging, hands-on, exciting, interactive, and outdoor activities. Until churches understand how men worship, learn, serve and live out their faith, then church will always have a shortage of men. As long as the church expects men to practice Christianity in the exact same fashion as women, the church will be perceived by men as a faith for females. Failure to respect the distinctions and uniqueness of the sexes will cause men to remain turned off to the church.

With the problem being common and the causes varied, the question becomes, "What are the solutions?" Not to over simplify the issue, but the bible does give us clear principles to guide us. From Joshua, to Jesus, to John, the principle has been the same: focus on men first and the families will follow. Many churches have focused much of its time, energy, and resources, to appeal and minister to women and children to the complete neglect of men. However, when reviewing scripture, the initial appeal was not to mothers and their children, but to the men and the fathers. Jesus spent time ministering to women and children, though his primary focus was on men—fathers, sons, and husbands. He spent over three years focused on 12 men, giving them examples, practical teaching, and hands on experience. As Marrow states, "He (Jesus) knew a truth we've forgotten: if you transform men, you transform the family, the community and the society. Draw a man to church, and you often get the family in the bargain." When Moses set up the tabernacle and David made preparations for the temple, they organized everything by the family, through the father.

Apostle John writes, "I write unto you, fathers, because ye have known him that is from the beginning. I write unto you, young men, because ye have overcome the wicked one. I write unto you, little children, because ye have known the Father. I have written unto you, fathers, because ye have known him that is from the beginning. I have written unto you, young men, because ye are strong, and the word of God abideth in you, and ye have overcome the wicked one" (I John 2:13-14, King James Version).

How can the church recapture multiple generations of men back into our congregations? When researching churches that have a strong male population, there are several things a church should consider: does the church have an active, relevant, and effective men's ministry? Are service times and ministry activities considerate of male schedules and outside interests? Do men have opportunities to serve in the church other than preaching, singing, ushering, or playing musical instruments? Does the men's ministry plan practical and recreational activities that appeal to men? With many churches having luxurious women's lounges and state of the art kid's zones, do the men in your church have a well-designed, designated area or "man cave" for fellowship? Does the church have men-only bible studies, small groups, Sunday school classes, or conferences that allow men to be open, honest, transparent, and accountable when it comes to male issues?

Are the men's ministry leaders a good example of being a masculine, hard-working, disciplined, and godly- son, husband, or father? For many men, the approach is simple: show me how it is done before you tell me how to do it!

Even at a time, when many boys grow up in single-parent households without fathers and are skeptical of male leadership, it is vital to have men-focused ministries. What better organization to fill that void in a young man's life and to assist a single mother in raising a young man, than the church. As young men grow up, role modeling and idolizing athletes and entertainers, seeking a challenge, acceptance and affirmation through sports teams, fraternities, military service and even gangs and other religions, it is that much more important for ministries to be relevant, practical, challenging, and authentic to men. Some men will benefit from a sermon to the masses, but as thinkers and doers, most will benefit even more from direct teaching, mentoring, recreation, and hands-on activities. Talking to the men while fishing on a boat will likely have a greater impact on them than the hour-long sermon given on Sunday—and be more enjoyable.

Quibbling, one might argue that all these suggestions sound great if you have a group of men in your church. However, rather than see a shortage of men in the church as an obstacle, see it as an opportunity. It is much easier to engage in mentoring and focused ministry when you have a few, than when you have many. While Jesus only had 12, he spent a substantial amount of time with three—James, John, and Peter. Twelve disciples became 70, the 70 disciples became 120 men and women in the upper room, and the 120 men and women in the upper room became 3000 souls added to the church on Pentecost. After the healing of the lame man at the gate called Beautiful, the scripture records "Howbiet many of them which heard the word believe; and the number of the MEN was about 5,000!" Acts 4:4 (King James Version).

Remember, there is a reason the scripture details the feeding of 5,000 men, not including women and children. Jesus taught the entire family with men leading the way. Imagine getting to a point where we could measure our weekly church attendance the same way; "We had _____ (insert number) men in service this week, not including women and children". With prayer and planning, a church can end the praying mantis spirit in its congregation.

Discussion Questions

(1) What percentage of your church members, or weekly church attendance, is made up of males?

(2) What roles and responsibilities do males participate in in your church?

(3) How often do the men at church get together for male-only bible study, recreation, or fellowship?

(4) Do men have a designated area for fellowship and learning in the church?

(5) How accessible are the men in leadership in the church to the other men in the congregation?

(6) How pro-active is your church in addressing, or correcting, some of the commonly identified reasons why men do not attend church?

(7) Review your most recent church calendar, how many activities were geared towards men? Women? Youth? Everyone?

(8) What percentage of men in your church come from single-parent or fatherless homes?

(9) What activities or initiatives have you provided to fill-the-gap or void that may exist from coming from father-less homes?

(10) How can you better motivate men who come to church, but are not necessarily involved in the church?

(11) What type of outreach activities or evangelism programs have been implemented specifically to minister to the men in your community?

References

Read more on Praying Mantis:

https://phys.org/news/2016-06-meal-mantis-cannibalism.html#jCp

https://www.thoughtco.com/praying-mantis-sex-and-male-cannibalism-1968472

https://www.huffingtonpost.com/2012/04/26/sexual-cannibalism-mantis-spider_n_1455276.html

Read more on why men don't go to church:
Fifteen Reasons Men Don't Attend Church
http://josephmattera.org/fifteen-reasons-men-dont-attend-church/

Why Men Hate Church
http://www1.cbn.com/churchandministry/why-men-hate-church

Church for Men
http://churchformen.com/

The Masculinity Myth: The Real Reason Men Don't Go to Church
http://www.patheos.com/blogs/evangelicalpulpit/2014/10/
the-masculinity-myth-the-real-reason-men-dont-go-to-
church/

Why do men stay away? by Thomas G. Long
https://www.christiancentury.org/article/2011-10/why-do-
men-stay-away

Why don't men go to church?
https://www.psephizo.com/life-ministry/why-dont-men-go-
to-church/

Why Men Hate Going to Church
By: David Murrow © 2005, 2011

No Man Left Behind: How to Build and Sustain A Thriving Disciple-Making Ministry for Every Man in Your Church
By: Patrick Morley, David Delk, and Brett Clemmer © 2006

CHAPTER 10

THE FISH TANK

Amanda returns home after a weekend visit to see her out of town parents. As a new owner of a fish tank, she is excited to see and feed her new pets. Perplexed, she finds one of her fish missing from the tank. Upon further examination, she notices something like a white cotton ball floating in the tank. She quickly realizes that her fish was not missing but dead. Amanda quickly goes online to learn how could a fish die and deteriorate in less than a weekend. After reading several articles, Amanda discovers that fish not only kill each other, but also eat other fish in a tank. Who would have thought that something that appeared to be so calm, serene, and peaceful could be so full of hostility, competition, and violence?

Typically, fish purchased as pets for a tank, such as guppies, goldfish, minnows, gouramis and plecos, are not known to be cannibalistic animals. However, when mixed with different fish in a tank, it appears that they take on a different nature, as cannibalistic animals. Various explanations, such as compatibility, competition, space limitations, water suitability, and scarcity of food, are given. Fish are very territorial and if other fish become threatened in any way, quarrels may break out, even with normally peaceful fish. Fish have been known to kill, and eat weak, sick, or deceased fish, that died of natural causes. As opportunistic predators, fish in the tank will quickly take advantage of the situation when a fish dies.

Some argue that these fish are not cannibalistic (eating its own kind), but opportunistic carnivores, eating other types of fish, no different than if they were in nature. However, some pet fish, such as guppies are known to be both prolific breeders as well as cannibalistic pet fish. Adult guppies will eat both their own fry (baby fish) and the fry of other fish, especially in crowded tanks. They will eat both healthy and unhealthy fish. The only way to preserve the fry is to place them in a tank separate from the adults until they are adult-sized. Otherwise, a few guppies may still be eaten, unless you are present at the moment of birth to catch all of them. It only takes a few days for the entire fry to be eaten by their parents or other members of the aquarium community.

The fish tank church is characterized as divided, territorial, nepotistic, political, competitive, and outright cliquish. A fish tank church is known by its divisions, dysfunction, and constant DRAMA! Fights between families, generations, ministers, musicians, auxiliary leaders, new and old members, traditional and contemporary members, loyalists of the previous pastor versus loyalists of the current pastor may happen, and down the list you go!

Similar to the fish tank, the church brings together people of diverse personalities, backgrounds, cultures, upbringings, and experiences, as well as levels of spiritual maturity and development. One of the beauties of the church is how God can bring various people together, often strangers, at a particular place and time, to form a church or congregation, but more importantly a family. Yet, the enemy knows that if he can exploit these differences, he can make the church turn against itself, rather than attack the true enemy.

In his farewell address, Pope Benedict said, "I am thinking particularly about the sins against the unity of the Church, about divisions in the body of the Church," and the need of "overcoming individualism and rivalry" because it has "disfigured" the face of the Church. Jesus, in John chapter 17 said this:

> *"I pray not only for them, but also for those who will believe in me through their word, so that they may all be one, as you, Father, are in me and I in you, that they also may be in us, that the world may believe that you sent me. And I have given them the glory you gave me, so that they may be one, as we are one, I in them and you in me, that they may be brought to perfection as one, that the world may know that you sent me, and that you loved them even as you loved me."*
>
> —(New American Bible Revised Edition)

Jesus makes it clear that the church must have unity for it to be successful in accomplishing its mission of winning souls to Christ. Jesus, in the previously quoted scripture said, "That the world may <u>believe</u> that you sent me." He later said, "And that the world may <u>know</u> that you sent me." In essence, the world will never believe or know Jesus while His church is divided.

As long as people are still in the flesh, conflict will arise. However, the problem is not the conflict, but in how conflict is handled and ultimately resolved. A preacher once remarked, "The devil gave up all of his tools, except for a wedge." Paul remarked, "Endeavoring to keep the unity of the spirit in the bond of peace" (Ephesians 4:3, King James Version). Paul understood that in order to achieve and maintain unity, unity in the church must be a priority and a constant endeavor.

Pet experts recommend ways to maintain unity in the fish tank—keep the water clean, keep the fish fed, maintain the right water temperature, and keep the salt levels balanced. From the bible, we can glean at least four ways to overcome disunity and overcome the fish tank syndrome: teaching (keep the fish fed), prayer (keep salt level balanced), fellowship (maintain the right temperature), and communication (keep the tank clean).

TEACHING

First, the topics of love, selflessness, preferring one another, unity, effective communication, and conflict resolution must be constantly taught in the church. With spirit-filled Christians, you would think this would come naturally, but as with anything else, it only becomes a part of the Christian practice if it is taught and emphasized on a consistent basis. In 1 Corinthians chapter 11, Paul taught on the unity and the operation of the body. Paul further wrote in chapter 13 on the definition of love in conjunction with the application of love. Similarly, with any team or organization, in order for unity to be achieved on a consistent high level, it must be taught and preached on a regular basis. Unity cannot be assumed or taken for granted. It must be taught.

FELLOWSHIP

Second, unity can be achieved through regular fellowship. You'd be surprised how people can worship together in the same church for years yet have very little meaningful interactions with each other or basic knowledge about one another. Unless a member is part of a sizable family in the church or is actively involved in a particular ministry, they may very well not know anyone outside of that ministry, family, or immediate circle of members. However, fellowship is not only biblical but essential for creating and maintaining unity. The more I know you, the more I understand you, and the better I am able to work with you.

Teams and organizations spend significant amounts of money on annual retreats, recreational activities, food functions, and team building exercises for this exact purpose. A recent article in Forbes magazine said,

> *"Despite its reputation for being, well, lame, team building is the most important investment you can make for your people. It builds trust, mitigates*

conflict, encourages communication, and increases collaboration. Effective team building means more engaged employees, which is good for company culture and boosting the bottom line."

It is hard to think of oneself as being a part of a family when people do not have a chance to know one another. Church cookouts, retreats, vacations, potluck dinners, and even bible studies that require people to get into unique groups can be tremendously beneficial. One pastor once remarked, "You would be surprised how much donuts and coffee before service or cookies and kool-aid after bible study can help create an atmosphere of fellowship and unity." It is no coincidence that in Acts, it specifically said that the saints "continued steadfastly in the apostle's doctrine and in <u>fellowship</u> and <u>breaking bread</u>." While it is important to schedule worship services and bible studies, it is also important for churches to be intentional and strategic in planning church-fellowship opportunities on a regular basis to foster unity within the congregation. For the church, the bottom line is not profits and sales, but souls being saved.

COMMUNICATION

Thirdly, unity can be achieved through good and frequent communication. Although it can be argued that too many meetings, with too many people, is one of the leading causes of disunity in a church, terminated communication is not the answer either. Some of your biggest church fights may come over what color the carpet should be in the nursery, but that does not mean all decisions should be done in isolation or behind closed doors. Indeed, too many cooks in the kitchen is a formula for disaster, but someone has to be in the kitchen if the food is to be cooked.

For churches to work in unity, the vision must be communicated clearly and regularly, and job descriptions and mission statements must be reviewed periodically.

Communication must also be a two-way street in that leaders should communicate to the congregation, but also the congregation should be able to communicate to leadership. As many things will never reach the pastor's desk, nor should it, members should be taught conflict resolution and how to communicate effectively with each other. Many of us have probably had someone leave the church because of a conflict with another member. The devil will plant grenades anywhere and anytime. This is why Jesus taught if any of you have an ought against your brother, leave your gift at the altar and reconcile quickly with your brother. You may have witnessed how a minor disagreement and misunderstanding can tear a church apart. Teaching people how to properly put out fires before they literally burn down the entire church, is essential.

Effective communication in the church also, at times, requires clarifying misunderstandings, mediating disputes, and correcting someone when they are wrong. In Matthew 20, when Jesus heard the dispute amongst the disciples as to who would be the greatest, Jesus immediately used the conflict as a teachable moment for his disciples. Avoiding conflict is never the best way to resolve conflict. Paul, upon hearing of Peter's behavior around Gentiles, when in the company of Jews, immediately confronted him about it. When the apostles were confronted with treatment of widows, they met, and God gave them the solution to ordain deacons. Likewise, when Paul hears of division in the Corinthian church over his leadership, he deals with the issue directly. Leaders cannot hide or abrogate authority when it comes to conflict resolution in the church.

PRAYER

Lastly, after all of the bible studies, fellowship opportunities, and rap sessions are over, the fourth key to creating and maintaining unity in the church is prayer. Prayer has a way of bringing unity to the body of Christ. Prayer creates the atmosphere for repentance, humility, self-denial, forgiveness, and healing. Ultimately, if there is a conflict in the church, what better arbitrator than the Holy Spirit. Hopefully after a period of prayer, two groups will either reach an agreement or agree to disagree, but in a peaceful manner. In many of our churches, unfortunately, we have very little time devoted to prayer.

During a two-hour worship service, perhaps five minutes is allocated for prayer. On our church schedules, many have eliminated prayer service from our weekly schedules. We should never forget that even Jesus prayed for his body to have unity. Jesus said, in John 17:20-21, "I pray not only for them, but also for those who will believe in me through their word, so that they may all be one, as you, Father, are in me and I in you, that they also may be in us..." (New American Bible Revised Edition). As stated earlier, Jesus makes it clear that the church must have unity for it to be successful in accomplishing its mission of winning souls to Christ. Praying for unity can't just be a cliche, but a constant practice in the church.

We further understand the power of unity in Ps. 133:1-2, "Behold, how good and how pleasant it is for brothers to dwell together in unity! It is like the precious oil upon the head, coming down upon the beard, even Aaron's beard, Coming down upon the edge of his robes" (New American Bible Revised Edition). When there is division and competition in the church, the oil cannot flow, and without the oil flowing, souls cannot be saved, set free or delivered.

We must never forget that the church is under constant attack and engaged in spiritual warfare. One of the oldest strategies of war is to divide and conquer. The enemy is looking to create distractions, chaos, and discord at the expense of souls being captured or killed. However, as Paul said, the weapons of our warfare are not carnal, but mighty through God for the pulling down of strongholds. The church has a superior weapon, and it is prayer.

Ultimately, some people will have to leave the congregation in order to reestablish unity. Sometimes when church leaders constantly make decisions in an attempt to keep certain individuals in the congregation happy, it can actually make the rest of the church unhappy and dissatisfied with the church and its leadership. In order to preserve harmonious coexistence of the fish in the tank, some fish will have to be removed. Paul warns us that, "...a little leaven leavens the whole lump? Cleanse out the old leaven that you may be a new lump" (1 Corinthians 5:6b-7a, English Standard Version). If so, it should be done in a loving, amendable, and positive manner. Some fish belong in their own tank.

Even though the tower of Babel was destroyed for improper motives, the principle of unity remains the same. If people come together for a common purpose, they can accomplish anything. This is even truer for a body of believers who come together for the purpose of God, trying to accomplish the mission of the church. Never forget the words of Jesus, when two or three are gathered in my name, touching and agreeing, nothing shall be impossible to them.

Discussion Questions

(1) Do you think the fish tank is an accurate metaphor for describing a church congregation? W hy or why not?

(2) What are some practical ways that church leaders can build unity and camaraderie with their church congregation?

(3) What reasons do you have as to why it seems to be such a ongoing struggle to maintain peace and unity in a church?

(4) In reviewing your church schedule over the last 12 months, how many services or events where planned primarily for the purpose of the church coming together for prayer?

(5) On a scale of 1-10, how would you rate your church as a praying church? What can be done immediately to maintain or improve your score?

(6) What scriptures address or provide examples of how church members should resolve conflicts with each other?

(7) Is it a sin to have a conflict with someone else in the church?

(8) What are the "right" and "wrong" reasons for a person to leave a church?

(9) What is the "right way" and the "wrong way" for a member to leave or relinquish their membership with a church?

(10) Under what circumstances or conditions (if ever) should someone be asked or encouraged to leave or relinquish their membership with a church?

References

Cannibal Fish Eating Each Other
https://www.myaquariumclub.com/cannibal-fish-eating-each-other-894816.html

How to Save Your Baby Guppies in a Community Tank
https://pets.thenest.com/save-baby-guppies-community-tank-3621.html

Do You Have Cannibalistic Fish?
Are Your Fish Eating Other Fish? Find Out Why
https://www.thespruce.com/cannibalistic-fish-1381212

Pope urging Church leaders to put aside rivalries
https://www.reuters.com/article/us-pope-resignation-rivalry/
pope-urging-church-leaders-to-put-aside-rivalries-
idUSBRE91D0XP20130214

Why Team Building Is The Most Important Investment
You'll Make
https://www.forbes.com/sites/brianscudamore/2016/03/09/
why-team-building-is-the-most-important-investment-
youll-make/#5cd69248617f

How To Deal With Conflict In The Church
https://www.whatchristianswanttoknow.com/how-to-deal-
with-conflict-in-the-church/#ixzz596Qm1UqB

6 Biblical Ways to Handle Disunity
http://pastors.com/6-biblical-ways-to-handle-disunity/

NATURE OF CHILDREN

In Matthew 18:6, Jesus says, "But whoso shall offend one of these little ones which believe in me, it were better for him that a millstone were hanged about his neck, and that he were drowned in the depth of the sea" (King James Version). A person may be an adult, physically, but may still be a child spiritually.

A baby cannot think for itself, so we must help it to develop the mind of Christ. A baby cannot communicate; they don't come out speaking English. The only thing they can do is cry. When people join our church, they don't know the language, they don't know the lingo, they don't know how to jump and shout on certain keys, but they have to be taught the language of the church.

Babies cannot stand and walk out of the womb. It takes time and many falls, bumps and bruises, before they learn how to walk and run. There will be people who join our churches, who are practicing alternative lifestyles. They'll tour our churches still cross-dressing, still shacking, still using drugs, but they want to be changed. They want to be delivered. The question is, "Will you take the time to teach them how to walk before Christ?"

A baby can't dress themselves. We must teach them the way of Holiness. A child can't feed themselves. We have to be willing to entertain their questions and to break down the word for them. You can't expect a child to eat a steak dinner out of the womb. But the Bible tells us to give them the sincere milk of the word of God.

Babies are vulnerable to diseases and to elements. A child can catch a cold in a heartbeat. We find that our children in the church have low resistance and a weak immune system. What does that mean? They're subject to trials, tribulations, tests and temptations. But the question is, "Are there nurses and doctors in the house that know how to nurse someone through, pray someone through, fast someone through, give them a word of encouragement?"

The last characteristic of a baby is that a baby is not born potty-trained, but a baby will poop on itself. Some children know better, but do it intentionally. There are some people that will sin intentionally, but for many kids, they don't know better. And so, there are many people who will join our churches and will get caught up in sin, relationships and addictions. The question is, "When they make a mistake or a mess, what do we do with them?" Sometimes, the poop is real nice and neat and other times you need to call Hazmat to assist with cleanup.

Most parents have experienced at least once in their life, when their child had to use the bathroom so badly that it was up their back, in their hair, down their leg, and oozing out of their onesie. It was all over their bed and all over the wall. In the same way, there are going to be children in the church that make a mess of everything.

But the question is, "When that baby is stinking, nasty, and dirty, do you throw it away, the diaper, or do you throw away the child?" We take the time to say, "Come here, baby, let me wash you up", "Come here, baby, let me put some lotion on you", "Come here baby, let me put some baby powder on. It's going to make you smell good", "Baby, can I put some new clothes on you?", but do we know how to treat the babies in our church?"

And so, the Lord is saying to the church, that we can't have the spirit of Pharaoh or Herod, killing all the babies. We must cultivate, train and develop our babies. It's not good enough just to invite and to witness to them, give them hospitality bags, and then, after weeks, months, or years, we have killed the baby, or the baby is nowhere to be found. Are we an abortion clinic or an incubator? Do we know how to take the preemie and bring them to full term? Are we a cradle that allows the baby time to learn and grow, a nursery that knows how to feed and to train our children? Are we a child development center that will teach the children the foundations of the Christian walk?

I leave you with this final observation from our initial passage. There was an agreement between two mothers to eat each other's child. However, after eating the first child, the mother of the second child made the decision to hide her child to keep it from being eaten. The reality is, many of us can do very little to correct past mistakes or missed opportunities; we can only focus on the future. The second mother made the decision that cannibalism must end. You too can make the decision that the cannibalism in our church is over and will never happen again. I believe with repentance, prayer, collaboration, and strategic thinking, we can change the nature of our churches and be the house of prayer for all people that God always intended for His church to be.

ABOUT THE AUTHOR

Bishop T. Travell Travis, Esq., serves as the founding pastor of City of Refuge Way of the Cross Church in Richmond, VA. Within the Way of the Cross Church of Christ International, he is a member of the board of bishops and trustee board. He also serves as general counsel and as president of its international youth department.

Dr. Travis is a native of Martinsville, Virginia. He received his B.A. from the University of Virginia with a double major in History and African American Studies and a minor in Religious Studies. He received his J.D. from Howard University School of Law.

Since 2003, Dr. Travis has been employed by the Hampton University School of Business. Dr. Travis teaches entrepreneurship and business law courses as a faculty member in the Center for Entrepreneurial Studies. From 2004-2017, Dr. Travis served as an assistant dean for the School of Business. He is a past recipient of the Hampton University Chancellor and Provost Teaching Innovation Award and the Hampton University Academic Excellence Award.

In 2005, Attorney Travis opened the Law Office of Travell Travis, P.L.C.; a general practice law firm with offices in Richmond and Hampton, Virginia. Attorney Travis is admitted to practice law in the Commonwealth of Virginia and the District of Columbia. He is a member of the Apostolic Law Association. He regularly presents seminars on church law and entrepreneurship. His educational videos on these subjects can be found on social media.

Bishop Travis is married to the former Sherina D. Mason, of Philadelphia, PA. They reside together in Richmond, Virginia, with their three daughters: Deonna, Janiyah, and Amiyah.

www.travelltravis.com

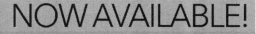

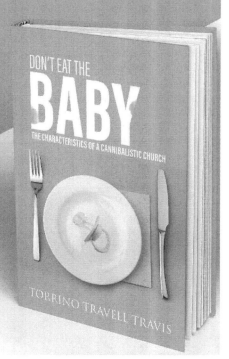